PRIMARY MATHEMATICS
Standards Edition

TEXTBOOK

Marshall Cavendish
Education

Blank

Original edition published under the title Primary Mathematics Textbook 5A
© 1983 Curriculum Planning & Development Division, Ministry of Education, Singapore
Published by Times Media Private Limited

This edition © 2008 Marshall Cavendish International (Singapore) Private Limited
© 2014 Marshall Cavendish Educaton Pte Ltd

Published by Marshall Cavendish Education
Times Centre, 1 New Industrial Road, Singapore 536196
Customer Service Hotline: (65) 6213 9444
US Office Tel: (1-914) 332 8888 | Fax: (1-914) 332 8882
E-mail: tmesales@mceducation.com
Website: www.mceducation.com

Marshall Cavendish Corporation
99 White Plains Road
Tarrytown, NY 10591
U.S.A.
Tel: (1-914) 332 8888
Fax: (1-914) 332 8882
E-mail: mcc@marshallcavendish.com
Website: www.marshallcavendish.com

First published 2008
Reprinted 2009, 2010, 2011, 2012 (twice), 2014, 2015, 2017, 2018

Primary Mathematics (Standards Edition) Textbook 5A
ISBN 978-0-7614-6985-8

Printed in Singapore

Primary Mathematics (Standards Edition) is adapted from Primary Mathematics Textbook 5A (3rd Edition), originally
developed by the Ministry of Education, Singapore. This edition contains new content developed by Marshall Cavendish
International (Singapore) Private Limited, which is not attributable to the Ministry of Education, Singapore.

We would like to acknowledge the Project Team from the Ministry of Education, Singapore, that developed the original
Singapore Edition:
Project Director: Dr Kho Tek Hong
Team Members: Hector Chee Kum Hoong, Liang Hin Hoon, Lim Eng Tann,
               Rosalind Lim Hui Cheng, Ng Hwee Wan, Ng Siew Lee
Curriculum Specialists: Christina Cheong Ngan Peng, Ho Juan Beng, Sin Kwai Meng

Our thanks to Richard Askey, Emeritus Professor of Mathematics (University of Wisconsin, Madison) and Madge Goldman,
President (Gabriella and Paul Rosenbaum Foundation), for their help and advice in the production of Primary Mathematics
(Standards Edition).

We would also like to recognize the contributions of Jennifer Kempe (Curriculum Advisor, Singapore Math Inc.®) and
Bill Jackson (Math Coach, School No. 2, Paterson, New Jersey) to Primary Mathematics (Standards Edition).

Mathematics Content Standards for California Public Schools reproduced by permission,California Department of Education,
CDE Press, 1430 N Street, Suite 3207, Sacramento, CA 95814.

PREFACE

PRIMARY MATHEMATICS **(Standards Edition)** is a complete program from the publishers of Singapore's successful *Primary Mathematics* series. Newly adapted to align with the Mathematics Framework for California Public Schools, the program aims to equip students with sound concept development, critical thinking and efficient problem-solving skills.

Mathematical concepts are introduced in the opening pages and taught to mastery through specific learning tasks that allow for immediate assessment and consolidation.

The **modeling method** enables students to visualize and solve mathematical problems quickly and efficiently.

The **Concrete → Pictorial → Abstract** approach enables students to encounter math in a meaningful way and translate mathematical skills from the concrete to the abstract.

The **pencil icon** ✏️ Exercise 18, pages 18-20 provides quick and easy reference from the Textbook to the relevant Workbook pages. The **direct correlation** of the Workbook to the Textbook facilitates focused review and evaluation.

New mathematical concepts are introduced through a **spiral progression** that builds on concepts already taught and mastered.

③ Factors and Multiples
Ali has 18 stamps. He arranges the stamps in sets of 3.

$18 = 3 \times 6$ 18 is a **multiple** of 3.

3 is a **factor** of 18.

18 can be divided by 3 exactly.

$$\begin{array}{r} 6 \\ 3\overline{)18} \\ \underline{18} \\ 0 \end{array}$$

Is 18 a **multiple** of 6?
Is 6 a **factor** of 18?

Is 4 a factor of 110?

As 110 cannot be divided by 4 exactly, 4 is not a factor of 110.

$$\begin{array}{r} 27 \\ 4\overline{)110} \\ \underline{8} \\ 30 \\ \underline{28} \\ 2 \end{array}$$

17

Metacognition is employed as a strategy for learners to monitor their thinking processes in problem solving. Speech and thought bubbles provide guidance through the thought processes, making even the most challenging problems accessible to students.

⑥ Fraction of a Set
Lihua bought 12 eggs. She used $\frac{2}{3}$ of them to bake a cake. How many eggs did she use?

Method 1:

Divide 12 eggs into 3 equal groups. 2 groups are shaded to show $\frac{2}{3}$.

$\frac{2}{3}$ of 12 =

She used eggs.

Method 2:   12

Draw a bar to represent 12 eggs. Divide the bar into 3 equal parts and shade 2 parts to show $\frac{2}{3}$.

3 units = 12
1 unit =
$\frac{2}{3}$ of 12 = 2 units =
She used eggs.

Method 3:
$\frac{2}{3} \times 12 = \frac{2 \times 12}{3}$

She used eggs.

67

The color patch is used to invite active student participation and to facilitate lively discussion about the mathematical concepts taught.

REVIEW 2

1. (a) What number is one thousand less than one million?
   (b) What number is one hundred thousand less than one hundred million?

2. Find the value of each of the following expressions.
   (a) $12 \div (6 - 2) + 7 \times 2 - 8$ (b) $20 - 8 \div 2 \times 4 + 1$
   (c) $6 \times (5 + 6) - 18 + 8$ (d) $(7 - 3) \times 3 + 9 + 3$

3. $51,283,000 = \square + 80,000 + 3000$

4. What is the greatest whole number that will make the statements true?
   (a) $75 + \square < 100$ (b) $\square - 97 < 100$

5. What is the smallest number that can be formed from the digits 7, 9, 0, 2, 6, and 5?

6. Mimi left home at 8:25 a.m. She returned home at 4:15 p.m. How long was she away from home?

7. What is the missing number in each $\square$?
   (a) $36 \times 25 = 9 \times \square$ (b) $7 \times 45 = 21 \times \square$
   (c) $25 \times 24 = 100 \times \square$ (d) $15 \times 18 = 3 \times \square$
   (e) $8 + 8 + 6 \times 2 = \square \times 6 + 28$ (f) $46 \times 7 = (40 \times \square) + (6 \times \square)$

8. Multiply.
   (a) 62×99 (b) 84×29 (c) 76×25

9. Add or subtract.
   (a) $698 + 83$ (b) $943 - 499$ (c) $1248 + 399$

10. Multiply.
    (a) 71×29 (b) 86×36 (c) 35×94
    (d) 258×24 (e) 574×62 (f) 392×44
    (g) 7067×39 (h) 6830×72 (i) 4872×44

49

Regular **reviews** in the Textbook provide consolidation of concepts learned.

GLOSSARY

Word	Meaning
approximation	The **approximation** of a number is the number obtained after we have rounded it to the nearest thousands, millions or billions. 2546 rounded to the nearest thousand is 3000. 2546 is **approximately** 3000.
billion	One **billion** is one thousand millions, or 1,000,000,000.
composite number	A **composite number** has factors other than 1 and itself. 6 is a composite number because its factors are 2 and 3 apart from 1 and itself.
equivalent ratios	**Equivalent ratios** are two or more ratios that have the same value. 1 : 2, 2 : 4 and 4 : 8 are **equivalent ratios**.
exponent	The **exponent** tells us how many times to multiply the base with itself. $4^3 = 4 \times 4 \times 4$ base exponent

154

The **glossary** effectively combines pictorial representation with simple mathematical definitions to provide a comprehensive reference guide for students.

CONTENTS

1 WHOLE NUMBERS

1 Billions

On September 1, 2006, the population of the world was 6,541,161,782.

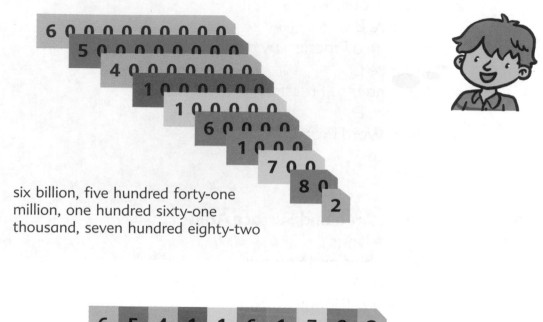

6 0 0 0 0 0 0 0 0 0
5 0 0 0 0 0 0 0 0
4 0 0 0 0 0 0 0
1 0 0 0 0 0 0
1 0 0 0 0 0
6 0 0 0 0
1 0 0 0
7 0 0
8 0
2

six billion, five hundred forty-one
million, one hundred sixty-one
thousand, seven hundred eighty-two

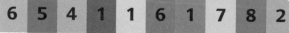

| 6 | 5 | 4 | 1 | 1 | 6 | 1 | 7 | 8 | 2 |

Billions			Millions			Thousands			Ones		
Hundreds	Tens	Ones	Hundreds	Tens	Ones	Hundreds	Tens	Ones	Hundreds	Tens	Ones
		6	5	4	1	1	6	1	7	8	2

Standard form: 6,541,161,782

Expanded form:

6,000,000,000 + 500,000,000 + 40,000,000 + 1,000,000 +
100,000 + 60,000 + 1000 + 700 + 80 + 2

Starting from the right, each group of 3 digits forms a **period**.
Commas separate the periods.

In words:

Six billion, five hundred forty-one million, one hundred
sixty-one thousand, seven hundred eighty-two

The value of the digit 1 is 1 × ⬜.

6,541,161,782 = ⬜ + 1782

4-digit numbers, such as 1782, can be written without a comma.

1. On July 1, 2006, the population of the United States was 295,734,134.

   (a) Write the number in words.
   (b) Write the number in expanded form.
   (c) The place value of 2 in 295,734,134 is hundred millions.
       What is the place value of 7?
   (d) What digit is in the ten millions place?
   (e) What digit is in the thousands place?

   (f) 295,734,134 is ⬜ more than 734,134.

2. Write the following numbers in words and in expanded form.

   (a) 340,600   (b) 50,493,400   (c) 34,034,005,182

3. The maximum distance from the sun to Uranus is about two billion, eight hundred seventy million kilometers. Write this number in figures.

4. (a) $3,000,000 + 400 + 4 =$ ▢

   (b) $60 + 1,000,000 + 5000 + 20,000,000 + 4 =$ ▢

5. (a) Ten thousand more than 345,045,000 is ▢ .

   (b) Ten million less than 2,934,300,200 is ▢ .

   (c) ▢ is one hundred less than 10,000,000.

   (d) ▢ is one hundred thousand more than 4,992,000.

6. The land area of the United States is 9,161,923 square kilometers. The land area of China is 9,326,410 square kilometers. Which country has more land area?

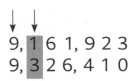
9, **1** 6 1, 9 2 3
9, **3** 2 6, 4 1 0

Starting from the left, we compare the digits in each place value, until we find 2 digits that are different.

7. Which number is smaller, 385,400,302 or 85,329,400?

8. Write >, <, or = in each ◯ .

   (a) 4,513,452 ◯ 4,513,452

   (b) 24,602,000,000 ◯ 26,402,000

Exercise 1, pages 5 - 6

❷ Approximation and Estimation

In 2005, 32,641,526 people attended the NCAA football games.

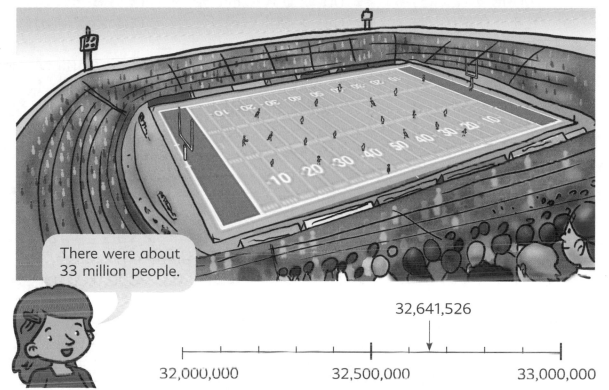

There were about 33 million people.

32,641,526

|—————|—————|—————|—————|—————|
32,000,000   32,500,000   33,000,000

Carla **rounds** 32,641,526 to the nearest million,

   32,641,526 ≈ 33,000,000

32,641,526 is **approximately** 33,000,000.

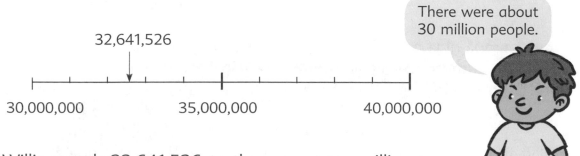

There were about 30 million people.

32,641,526

|—————|—————|—————|—————|
30,000,000   35,000,000   40,000,000

Willie rounds 32,641,526 to the nearest ten million.

   32,641,526 ≈ 30,000,000

32,641,526 is **approximately** 30,000,000.

1. In 2005, attendance for the Wimbledon Championship was 467,188.
Round the number to the nearest thousand.

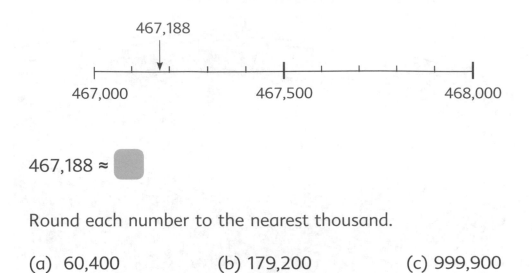

467,188 ≈ ⬜

Round each number to the nearest thousand.

(a) 60,400   (b) 179,200   (c) 999,900

2. Round 2,750,000 to the nearest hundred thousand.

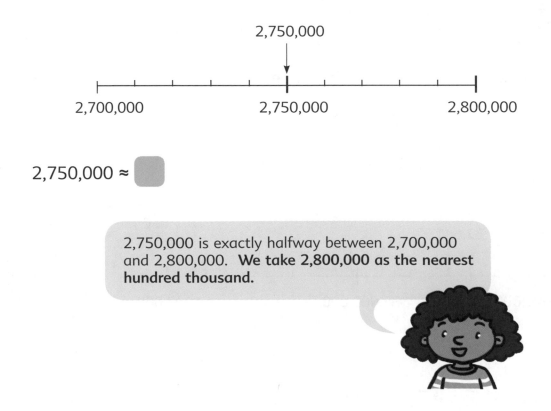

2,750,000 ≈ ⬜

2,750,000 is exactly halfway between 2,700,000 and 2,800,000. **We take 2,800,000 as the nearest hundred thousand.**

3. Round 172,866,529 to the nearest million.

What digit is in the millions place?

↓
1 7 2, 8 6 6, 5 2 9

What digit is in the next lower place?

↓
1 7 2, 8 6 6, 5 2 9

Do we round up or down?

172,866,529 is [ ] rounded to the nearest million.

> To round a number, we look at the digit in the next lower place value. If it is less than 5, we round down. If it is 5 or greater, we round up.

4. Round each number to the place named.
    (a)   285,043: ten thousands
    (b)   25,590,430: millions
    (c)   5,996,450,012: hundred millions

5. Round 4,569,325 to the place named.
    (a)   tens
    (b)   hundreds
    (c)   thousands
    (d)   ten thousands
    (e)   hundred thousands
    (f)   millions

Exercise 2, pages 7 - 8

6. Find the value of 180,000 ÷ 3.

180,000 ÷ 3 = ☐

180 thousands ÷ 3 = 60 thousands

7. Find the value of
   (a) 2,700,000 + 600,000
   (b) 4,500,000 − 800,000
   (c) 700,000 × 4
   (d) 350,000 ÷ 5

8. Estimate the value of 293,400 × 6.

293,400 × 6 ≈ 300,000 × 6
          = ☐

9. Estimate the value of 542,300 ÷ 8.

542,300 ÷ 8 ≈ 560,000 ÷ 8
          = ☐

480,000 and 560,000 are multiples of 8. Take 542,300 ≈ 560,000.

10. Round each number to the nearest 100,000.
    Then estimate the value of
    (a) 639,043 + 599,216
    (b) 7,812,300 + 896,900
    (c) 830,700 − 426,500
    (d) 4,562,718 − 732,491

11. Estimate the value of
    (a) 380,600 × 9
    (b) 979,400 × 5
    (c) 478,500 ÷ 6
    (d) 378,200 ÷ 4

14

Exercise 3, pages 9 - 11

PRACTICE A

1. Write the following in standard form.
   (a) 45 millions 8 hundreds 9 tens
   (b) 123 thousands 4 tens 5 ones
   (c) 1600 thousands 8 hundreds
   (d) 4 millions 230 thousands
   (e) Eight billion
   (f) Forty-six billion, four hundred twenty thousand, two

2. Write the following in words.
   (a) 945,025
   (b) 45,045,200
   (c) 100,100,001
   (d) 123,000,000,123

3. Arrange the numbers in increasing order.
   (a) 345,453,435   435,453,345   453,435,345   354,345,543
   (b) 6,293,400   26,934,000   36,349,000   239,693,000

4. (a) What number is 1 less than ten million?
   (b) What number is 100 less than ten million?
   (c) What number is 1000 less than ten million?
   (d) What number is 10,000 less than ten million?

5. Round 458,960,405 to the place given.
   (a) tens
   (b) ten thousands
   (c) ten million
   (d) hundreds
   (e) hundred thousands
   (f) hundred millions

6. A comet traveled 99,650,000 miles. Round this distance to the nearest million miles.

7. This table shows the number of people living in three towns.

	Number of people
Town A	179,920
Town B	176,392
Town C	170,500

   (a) Round the number of people in each town to the nearest 1000.
   (b) Use your answers in part (a) to estimate the total number of people in the 3 towns.

8. Round each number to the nearest 1000.
   Then estimate the value of
   (a) 32,370 + 4959
   (b) 24,890 + 5016
   (c) 48,207 − 9864
   (d) 54,500 − 6892

9. Estimate the value of
   (a) 8659 × 4
   (b) 6023 × 9
   (c) 7080 ÷ 8
   (d) 4378 ÷ 7

3 Factors and Multiples

Ali has 18 stamps. He arranges the stamps in sets of 3.

$$18 = 3 \times 6$$

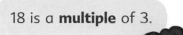

18 is a **multiple** of 3.

3 is a **factor** of 18.

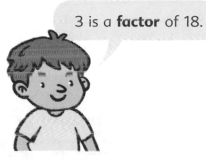

$$\begin{array}{r} 6 \\ 3\overline{)18} \\ 18 \\ \hline 0 \end{array}$$

18 can be divided by **3** exactly.

Is 18 a **multiple** of 6?

Is 6 a **factor** of 18?

1. Is 4 a factor of 110?

$$\begin{array}{r} 27 \\ 4\overline{)110} \\ 8 \\ \hline 30 \\ 28 \\ \hline 2 \end{array}$$

Since 110 cannot be divided by 4 exactly, 4 is not a factor of

2. Find the factors of 84.

$$84 = 1 \times 84$$
$$= 2 \times 42$$
$$= 3 \times 28$$
$$= \ldots$$

3. Find the factors of each number.
   (a) 36   (b) 64   (c) 124   (d) 144

4. Is 6 a common factor of 54 and 132?

5. List the common factors of 12 and 20.
   What is the **greatest common factor** of 12 and 20?
   Factors of 12 : 1, 2, 3, 4, 6, 12
   Factors of 20 : 1, 2, 4, 5, 10, 20

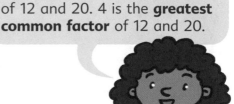

1, 2 and 4 are common factors of 12 and 20. 4 is the **greatest common factor** of 12 and 20.

6. List the first 12 multiples of 5.   5, 10, 15, 20, ...

7. Is 48 a common multiple of 6 and 8?

8. Give a common multiple of 5 and 8.
   Multiples of 5 : 5, 10, 15, 20, 25, 30, 35, **40** ...
   Multiples of 8 : 8, 16, 24, 32, **40** ...

40 is a common multiple of 5 and 8. It is also the **lowest common multiple** of 5 and 8.

9. Give a common multiple of 3, 4 and 9.

Exercise 4, pages 12 - 13

④ Prime Factorization

Find all the prime numbers to 50.

First, list the numbers from 1 to 50:

A **prime number** is a number greater than 1. It has exactly two factors, 1 and the number itself.

1	2	3	4	5	6	7	8	9	10
11	12	13	14	15	16	17	18	19	20
21	22	23	24	25	26	27	28	29	30
31	32	33	34	35	36	37	38	39	40
41	42	43	44	45	46	47	48	49	50

Cross out 1, since it is not a prime number.

A **composite number** has at least two factors that are not 1. The number 1 is neither prime nor composite.

Except for 2 itself, cross out all the remaining numbers that have 2 as a factor.

Except for 3 itself, cross out all the remaining numbers that have 3 as a factor.

Why do we not have to cross out numbers that have 4 as a factor?

Except for 5 itself, cross out all the remaining numbers that have 5 as a factor.

Why do we not have to cross out numbers that have 6 as a factor?

Except for 7 itself, cross out all the remaining numbers that have 7 as a factor.

Why can we stop after crossing out numbers that have 7 as a factor?

List the numbers to 50 that have not been crossed out. These are the prime numbers less than 50.

What do you notice about the ones digits of these prime numbers?

There are some pairs of prime numbers whose difference is two. These are called twin primes. 3 and 5 are twin primes. List all the twin primes less than 50.

1. The factors of 12 are 1, 2, 3, 4, 6 and 12. Which factors of 12 are prime factors?

Prime factors are any factors of a number which are prime numbers.

2 Express 12 as a product of prime factors only.

12 = ☐ × ☐ × ☐

3. Find the prime factorization of 72.

Prime factorization is the process of factoring a composite number into its prime factors.

Method 1: Use a factor tree.

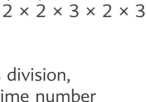

```
        72                      72
       /  \                    /  \
      8    9                  12    6
     /\    /\                /\    /\
    4  2  3  3              4  3  2  3
   /\                      /\
2 × 2 × 2 × 3 × 3        2 × 2 × 3 × 2 × 3
```

Method 2: Use continuous division, starting with the lowest prime number that is a factor.

Remember:
2 is a factor of all even numbers.
3 is a factor of a number if the sum of its digits is a multiple of 3.
5 is a factor of a number if the last digit is 0 or 5.

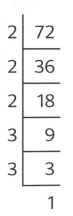

```
2 | 72
2 | 36
2 | 18
3 |  9
3 |  3
  |  1
```

72 = 2 × 2 × 2 × 3 × 3

4. Find the prime factorization of the following numbers.
   (a) 15   (b) 50   (c) 36

5. Show the prime factorization of 72 using exponents. Start with the lowest prime number.

   $72 = 2 \times 2 \times 2 \times 3 \times 3 = 2^3 \times 3^2$

$2^3 = 2 \times 2 \times 2$

2^3 ← exponent

2^3 ↖ base

The exponent tells us how many times to multiply the base with itself.

6. (a) 2^4 is read as **2 to the fourth power**. What is its value?

   $2^4 = 2 \times 2 \times 2 \times 2 = $ ▢

   (b) Find the value of 4 to the third power.

7. Find the value of the following.
   (a) 3^3
   (b) 7^2
   (c) $3^3 \times 7^2$
   (d) 1^7

8. Rewrite, using exponents.
   (a) $2 \times 2 \times 2 \times 5 \times 5 \times 5$
   (b) $5 \times 3 \times 3 \times 5 \times 7$
   (c) $11 \times 7 \times 11 \times 7$

9. Show the prime factorization using exponents.
   (a) 60
   (b) 24
   (c) 100

21

Exercise 5, pages 14 - 15

PRACTICE B

1. Find all the factors of each number.
   (a) 56   (b) 72   (c) 108   (d) 120

2. Give the greatest common factor for each pair of numbers.
   (a) 12 and 72   (b) 18 and 57   (c) 48 and 84

3. List the first four multiples of each number.
   (a) 5   (b) 7   (c) 8   (d) 9

4. Give the lowest common multiple of each set of numbers.
   (a) 3 and 5   (b) 6 and 8   (c) 4, 6, and 9

5. Find the missing factors.

   (a) $\boxed{} \times 6 = 84$ (b) $5 \times \boxed{} = 120$

   (c) $\boxed{} \times 3 = 99$ (d) $\boxed{} \times 5 = 75$

   (e) $4 \times \boxed{} = 116$ (f) $6 \times \boxed{} = 132$

6. Which of the following numbers have 2 as a factor?
   (a) 42   (b) 63   (c) 128   (d) 349

7. Which of the following numbers have 3 as a factor?
   (a) 92   (b) 69   (c) 252   (d) 413

8. Which of the following numbers have 5 as a factor?
   (a) 40   (b) 82   (c) 195   (d) 660

9. Express the following using exponents.
   (a) $5 \times 5 \times 11 \times 11 \times 11$ (b) $2 \times 2 \times 13 \times 13 \times 31 \times 2$
   (c) $5 \times 3 \times 19 \times 3 \times 19 \times 5 \times 2$

10. Find the value of each of the following.
    (a) $2^4 \times 3^3$ (b) $2^2 \times 7^2$ (c) $11^2 \times 3^2$

11. Express each of the following as a product of prime factors using exponents.
    (a) 28   (b) 54   (c) 88   (d) 108

22

⑤ Multiplying by Tens, Hundreds or Thousands

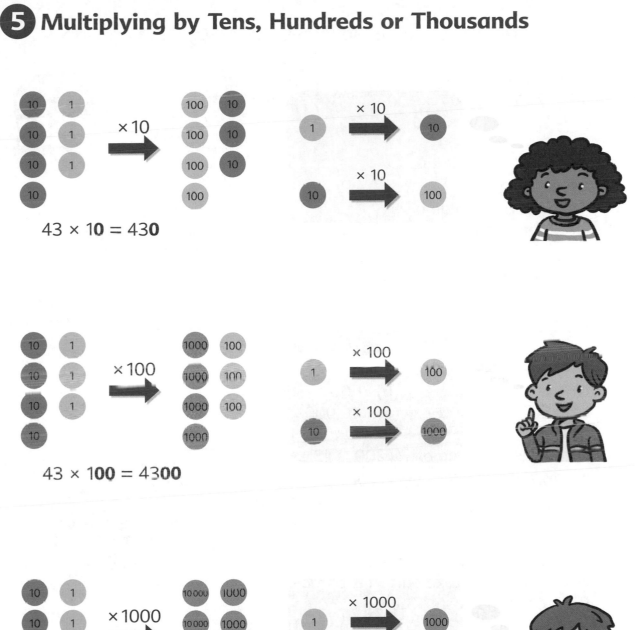

$$43 \times 10 = 430$$

$$43 \times 100 = 4300$$

$$43 \times 1000 = 43,000$$

1. Multiply.
   (a) 3280 × 10   (b) 100 × 53,600   (c) 630 × 1000

2. Multiply 16 by 700.

   16 × **7**00 = 16 × 7 × **1**00

            = 112 × **1**00

            = 11,2**00**

   Multiply 16
   by 7 first.

   $$\begin{array}{r} 16 \\ \times \quad 7 \\ \hline 112 \end{array}$$

3. Multiply 485 by 3.
   Then find the value of
   (a) 485 × 30   (b) 485 × 300   (c) 485 × 3000

4. Multiply 45,000 by 6.
   Then find the value of
   (a) 45,000 × 60   (b) 45,000 × 600   (c) 45,000 × 6000

5. Multiply.
   (a) 200 × 5000   (b) 600 × 9000   (c) 800 × 60,000
   (d) 500 × 20,000   (e) 40,000 × 600   (f) 2000 × 500,000

6. Estimate the value of 70,200 × 190.

   70,200 × 190 ≈ 70,**000** × 2**00**

   70,200 ≈ 70,000
   190 ≈ 200

   = ▢

7. Mrs. Bates needs 543 costumes for
   her students to take part in a parade.
   Each costume costs $35. Give a quick
   estimate of the total cost of the costumes.

   35 × 543 ≈ 4**0** × 5**00**

            = 20,**000**

   The total cost is about $20,**000**.

8. Estimate the value of
   (a) 529 × 340   (b) 7500 × 386   (c) 7804 × 590

Exercise 6, pages 16 - 17

6 Dividing by Tens, Hundreds or Thousands

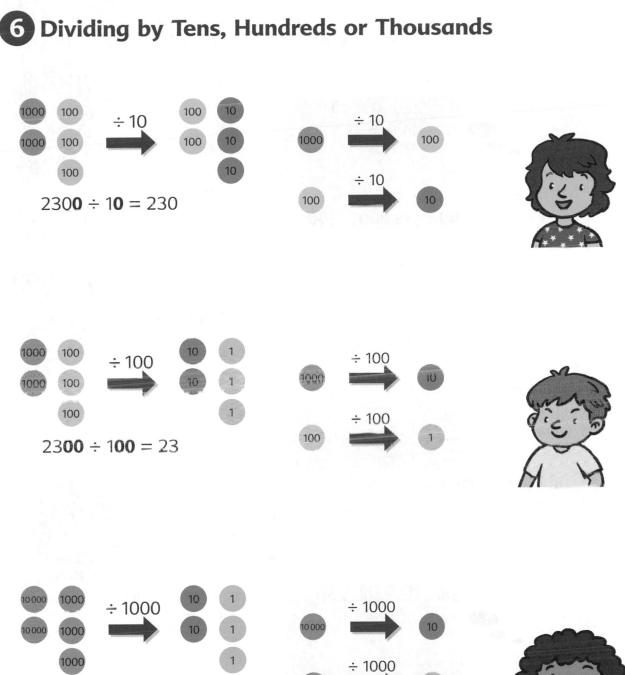

$2300 \div 10 = 230$

$2300 \div 100 = 23$

$23{,}000 \div 1000 = 23$

1. Divide.
   (a) $5200 \div 10$ (b) $74{,}000 \div 100$ (c) $4{,}000{,}000 \div 1000$

2. (a) Divide 15,000 by 30. $15{,}000 \div 30$

   $$15{,}00\mathbf{0} \div \mathbf{3}0 = 15{,}00\mathbf{0} \div \mathbf{1}0 \div 3$$
   $$= 1500 \div 3$$
   $$= 500$$

   (b) Divide 15,000 by 300. $15{,}000 \div 300$

   $$15{,}0\mathbf{00} \div \mathbf{3}00 = 15{,}0\mathbf{00} \div \mathbf{1}00 \div 3$$
   $$= 150 \div 3$$
   $$= 50$$

   (c) Divide 15,000 by 3000. $15{,}000 \div 3000$

   $$15{,}\mathbf{000} \div \mathbf{3}000 = 15{,}\mathbf{000} \div \mathbf{1}000 \div 3$$
   $$= 15 \div 3$$
   $$= 5$$

3. Divide.
   (a) $2800 \div 40$ (b) $640{,}000 \div 800$ (c) $20{,}000{,}000 \div 5000$

4. Estimate the value of $29{,}920 \div 380$.

   $29{,}920 \div 380 \approx 28{,}000 \div 400$ $29{,}920 \approx 28{,}000$
   $= \boxed{}$ $380 \approx 400$

5. Maria paid $959 for 33 copies of a software. Give a quick estimate of the cost per copy.

   $$959 \div 33 \approx 900 \div 30$$
   $$= 30$$

   The cost per copy was about $30.

6. Estimate the value of
   (a) $63{,}980 \div 81$ (b) $22{,}050 \div 340$ (c) $63{,}800 \div 6700$

26    Exercise 7, pages 18 - 19

PRACTICE C

1. Multiply.
   (a) 238 × 10
   (b) 700 × 100
   (c) 37 × 1000
   (d) 10 × 400
   (e) 100 × 280
   (f) 1000 × 520

2. Multiply 56 by 7.
   Then find the value of
   (a) 56 × 70
   (b) 56 × 700
   (c) 56 × 7000

3. Multiply 75 by 9.
   Then find the value of
   (a) 75 × 90
   (b) 75 × 900
   (c) 75 × 9000

4. Divide 72 by 8.
   Then find the value of
   (a) 720,000 ÷ 80
   (b) 720,000 ÷ 800
   (c) 720,000 ÷ 8000

5. Divide 900 by 6.
   Then find the value of
   (a) 90,000 ÷ 60
   (b) 90,000 ÷ 600
   (c) 90,600 ÷ 600

6. Divide.
   (a) 360 ÷ 90
   (b) 7600 ÷ 40
   (c) 90,600 ÷ 600
   (d) 4080 ÷ 80
   (e) 35,000,000 ÷ 500
   (f) 41,200,000 ÷ 4000

7. There are 426 people attending a conference. The cost per person for a catered lunch is $38.75. Give an estimate of the cost to serve all the people at the conference.

8. A zoo wants to estimate how much it would cost to ship some hippopotamuses to a new location. An adult hippopotamus weighs an average of 5710 pounds. The zoo has 6 full-grown hippos and 2 half-grown hippos.
   (a) Estimate the total weight of these hippos.
   (b) If shipping costs 53 cents per pound, estimate how much it will cost to ship the hippos.

9. A school has $4300 to spend on new computers. Each computer costs $799. Estimate the number of computers the school can buy.

REVIEW 1

1. (a) Write 8,574,932 in expanded form.

   (b) The digit 7 is in the ⬜ place.

   (c) The value of the digit 8 is ⬜.

2. Write in standard form.
   (a) 368 thousands 7 hundreds
   (b) 2 millions 732 thousands
   (c) 74 billions 50 millions 4 ones
   (d) Sixty-six hundred thousand, six hundred six

3. $95,087,000 = 90,000,000 + $ ⬜ $+ 80,000 + 7000$

4. A plane traveled 580 mi. Round this distance to the nearest 100 miles.

5. Estimate the value of
   (a) 381×12 (b) 7706×220
   (c) 5106×234 (d) 667×4850
   (e) $6250 \div 78$ (f) $20,769 \div 36$
   (g) $382,700 \div 940$ (h) $61,050 \div 730$

6. What are the factors of 32?

7. What are the common factors of 30 and 45?

8. List the first six multiples of 7.

9. What is the smallest number that can be divided by 3, 6, and 8 exactly?

10. Find the missing number: ⬜ $\div 7 = 35$ R 3

11. Write a number less than one million that has 7 in both the hundred thousands place and the tens place.

12. What is the sum of the first four multiples of 6?

13. Find the sum of the prime numbers between 1 and 10.

14. Write the prime factorization of the following numbers.
    (a) 96   (b) 105   (c) 120

Review 1, pages 20 - 21

2 MORE CALCULATIONS WITH WHOLE NUMBERS

1 Calculations with Parentheses

Shelby collects glass figurines. She has 6 of them displayed on the mantelpiece and the rest of them displayed in a glass case with 4 shelves. Each shelf has 8 glass figurines. How many figurines does she have?

$$6 + 4 \times 8 = 6 + 32$$
$$= \boxed{}$$

Shelby has $\boxed{}$ glass figurines.

> **Order of Operations**: Do multiplication or division from left to right, then addition or subtraction from left to right.

Briana collects postcards from the places she has visited. For each place she has visited, she collects 6 cards with scenic places on them and 4 with native animals. So far, she has collected cards from 8 places. How many postcards does she have?

Can we use the same expression we used for Shelby's collection?

To show that we want to add the total number of postcards from each place first, we use parentheses.

> An expression has numbers and operation signs $(+, -, \times, \div)$. It does not have an equal sign.

$$(6 + 4) \times 8 = 10 \times 8$$
$$= \boxed{}$$

Briana has $\boxed{}$ postcards.

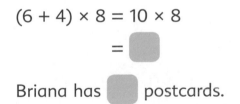

Compute the expression in parentheses first.

29

1. Find the value of $7 + 4 + 5 + 3 + 8 + 6$.

   $7 + 4 + 5 + 3 + 8 + 6 = 20 + 5 + 8$

   $= \square$

   > If the expression has only addition, I can add in any order.
   >
   > $7 + 4 + 5 + 3 + 8 + 6$

2. Find the value of $50 \times 28 \times 2$.

   $50 \times 28 \times 2 = 100 \times 28$

   $= \square$

   > If the expression has only multiplication, I can multiply in any order.
   >
   > $50 \times 28 \times 2$

3. Find the value of each of the following expressions.
   (a) $30 + 25 + 20$
   (b) $8 + 5 + 75 + 20 + 25$
   (c) $45 + 65 + 45 + 35$
   (d) $35 + 30 + 15 + 70$
   (e) $20 \times 35 \times 5$
   (f) $86 \times 25 \times 4$
   (g) $2 \times 30 \times 15$
   (h) $8 \times 4 \times 240 \times 2$

4. Find the value of $160 \div (4 + 2 \times 8) - 6$.

   $160 \div (4 + \underline{2 \times 8}) - 6$
   $= 160 \div (\underline{4 + 16}) - 6$
   $= \underline{160 \div 20} - 6$
   $= 8 - 6$
   $= \square$

   > If the expression has different kinds of operations, use the order of operations.

5. Find the value of $3 + 6 \times (5 + 4) \div 3 - 7$.

   $3 + 6 \times (5 + 4) \div 3 - 7$

   $= 3 + 6 \times \square \div 3 - 7$

   $= 3 + \square \div 3 - 7$

   $= 3 + \square - 7$

   $= \square - 7$

   $= \square$

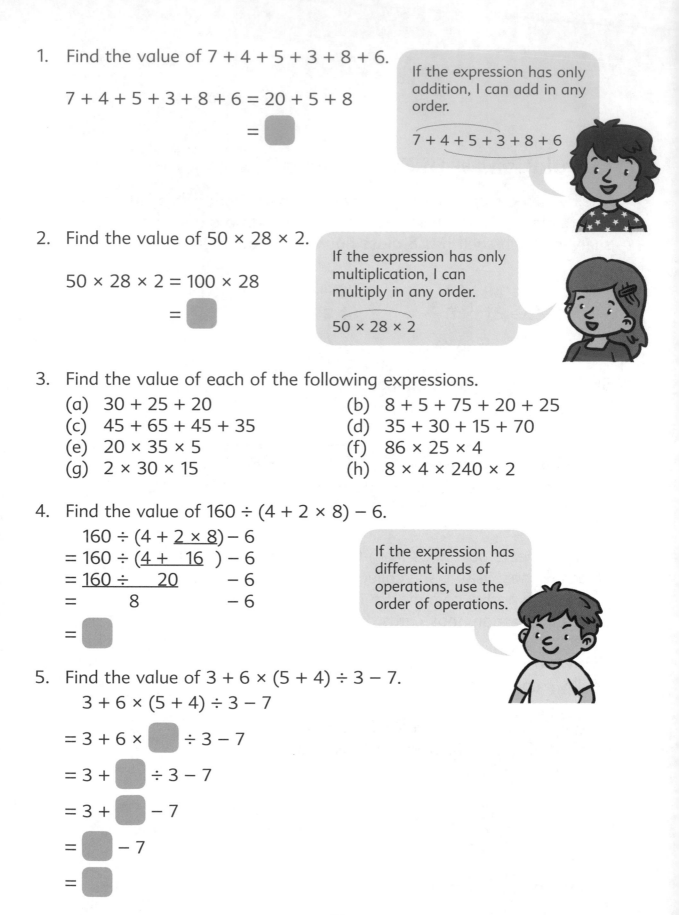

Find the value of each of the following expressions.

6. (a) 372 − (45 − 29) (b) 372 − 45 + 29
   (c) 372 − 45 − 29 (d) 372 − (45 + 29)
   (e) 128 ÷ 4 ÷ 2 (f) 128 ÷ (4 × 2)
   (g) 128 ÷ 4 × 2 (h) 128 ÷ (4 ÷ 2)

7. (a) 9 + 6 × (8 − 5) (b) 5 × 8 + 6 ÷ 6 − 12 × 2
   (c) (14 − 5) ÷ (9 − 6) (d) 9 − 5 ÷ (8 − 3) × 2 + 6

Exercise 1, pages 22 - 23

8. Briana has 6 scenic postcards and 4 animal postcards from each of the 8 places that she has visited. Show the number of postcards Briana has with an array.

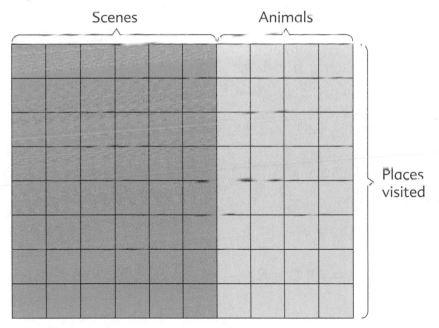

Scenes   Animals   Places visited

Find the total number of postcards.

Method 1:   **Method 2:**
(6 + 4) × 8   (6 × 8) + (4 × 8)

Do both methods give the same answer?

31

9. Find the value of
   (a) $(10 - 4) \times 3$
   (b) $(10 \times 3) - (4 \times 3)$

10. Find the missing numbers.
    (a) $(20 + 5) \times 3 = (20 \times \boxed{}) + (5 \times \boxed{})$

    (b) $(50 - 7) \times 8 = (\boxed{} \times 8) - (\boxed{} \times 8)$

    (c) $7 \times (4 + 3) = (7 \times \boxed{}) + (7 \times \boxed{})$

    (d) $3 \times (12 - 2) = (3 \times 12) - (3 \times \boxed{})$

    (e) $(3 \times 4) + (3 \times 5) = 3 \times (4 + \boxed{})$

    (f) $(10 \times 72) - (10 \times 28) = 10 \times (72 - \boxed{})$

11. Find the missing numbers.
    (a) $(20 + 4) \times 3 = (20 \times 3) + (\boxed{} \times 3)$

    (b) $24 \times 3 = (20 \times \boxed{}) + (4 \times \boxed{})$

    (c) $36 \times 8 = (\boxed{} \times 8) + (6 \times 8)$

    (d) $(70 - 1) \times 4 = (70 \times \boxed{}) - (1 \times \boxed{})$

    (e) $69 \times 4 = (70 \times \boxed{}) - (1 \times \boxed{})$

    (f) $99 \times 8 = (100 \times 8) - (\boxed{} \times 8)$

Exercise 2, page 24

PRACTICE A

1. Write a single expression for the following situation. Then solve the expression.

    The cost of going to a musical is $12 for adults and $8 for children under 18. A class of 20 students, along with one teacher and two parent helpers are going to the musical. There is a $20 discount for a group of at least 10 people. What will be the total cost?

2. Find the value of each expression.
    (a) 31 + 29 + 32 + 28
    (b) 194 + 31 + 9 + 8
    (c) 5 + 43 + 3 + 57 + 8 + 2
    (d) 500 × 7 × 2 × 30
    (e) 150 × 4 × 2 × 30

3. Find the value of
    (a) 28 ÷ (3 + 1) − 6   (b) 8 + (9 − 5) ÷ 2
    (c) 8 − 20 ÷ (5 × 4)   (d) 6 × (3 + 2) − 8
    (e) (16 − 4) ÷ (9 − 5)   (f) 50 − (9 + 7 × 4) + 10
    (g) 20 ÷ (3 + 2) × 3   (h) 10 − (2 − 6 ÷ 3) + 8
    (i) 2 × 3 − 8 ÷ 8 + 5   (j) 88 − 8 × 6 ÷ 3 − 80 ÷ 8 × 7

4. Find the missing numbers.
    (a) 14 × (3 + 6) = (14 × 3) + (14 × ☐)

    (b) 20 × (100 − 15) = (☐ × 100) − (☐ × 15)

    (c) (☐ + 6) × 5 = (3 × 5) + (6 × 5)

    (d) (52 − ☐) × 10 = (52 × ☐) − (2 × 10)

5. Write >, <, or = in each ⬤ .

    (a) (5 + 8) × 6 ⬤ (5 × 6) + (6 × 6)

    (b) 32 × (25 + 15) ⬤ (40 × 25) + (32 × 15)

    (c) 8 × (4 + 3) ⬤ (8 × 3) + (8 × 4)

2 Methods for Mental Calculation

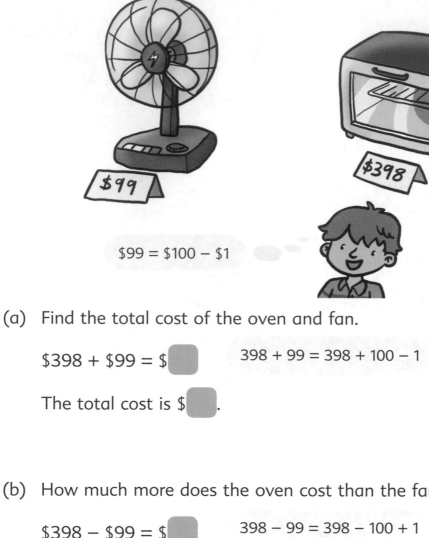

$99 = $100 − $1

(a) Find the total cost of the oven and fan.

$398 + $99 = $⬜   398 + 99 = 398 + 100 − 1

The total cost is $⬜.

(b) How much more does the oven cost than the fan?

$398 − $99 = $⬜   398 − 99 = 398 − 100 + 1

The oven costs $⬜ more than the fan.

(c) How much do 3 such fans cost?

$99 × 3 = $⬜   99 × 3 = 100 × 3 − 3

3 fans cost $⬜.

Add.

1. (a) 299 + 42   (b) 152 + 399   (c) 699 + 311
   (d) 39 + 201   (e) 301 + 269   (f) 509 + 401

2. (a) 283 + 107   (b) 314 + 206   (c) 635 + 305
   (d) 467 + 230   (e) 639 + 450   (f) 164 + 240

Subtract.

3. (a) 307 − 99   (b) 417 − 99   (c) 635 − 99
   (d) 433 − 299   (e) 509 − 399   (f) 789 − 499

4. (a) 785 − 450   (b) 654 − 330   (c) 872 − 470
   (d) 400 − 53   (e) 200 − 48   (f) 600 − 75

Exercise 3, pages 25 - 26

5. (a) Multiply 45 by 3.

$$45 \times 3 = 10 \times 3 + 5 \times 3$$
$$= 120 + 15$$
$$= \boxed{}$$

$$4\,5 \times 3 = 4\,0 \times 3 + 5 \times 3$$

   (b) Multiply 45 by 30.

$$45 \times 30 = 45 \times 3 \times 10$$
$$= 135 \times 10$$
$$= \boxed{}$$

6. Multiply.
   (a) 74 × 2   (b) 48 × 3   (c) 67 × 4
   (d) 36 × 7   (e) 94 × 5   (f) 83 × 6
   (g) 36 × 20   (h) 25 × 40   (i) 76 × 50
   (j) 62 × 70   (k) 43 × 60   (l) 29 × 80

7. Multiply 38 by 41.

$$38 \times 41 = 38 \times 40 + 38$$
$$= 1520 + 38$$
$$= \boxed{}$$

8. Multiply.
   (a) 45×11 (b) 26×51 (c) 18×61
   (d) 69×31 (e) 71×71 (f) 35×81

9. (a) Multiply 43 by 99.

   $$43 \times 99 = 43 \times 100 - 43$$
   $$= 4300 - 43$$
   $$= \boxed{}$$

   (b) Multiply 76 by 49.
   $$76 \times 49 = 76 \times 50 - 76$$
   $$= 3800 - 76$$
   $$= \boxed{}$$

10. Multiply.
    (a) 56×99 (b) 72×99 (c) 99×84
    (d) 75×59 (e) 37×39 (f) 69×56

11. Multiply 24 by 25.

    $$24 \times 25 = 6 \times 4 \times 25$$
    $$= 6 \times 100$$
    $$= \boxed{}$$

    $4 \times 25 = 100$

12. Multiply.
    (a) 16×25 (b) 28×25 (c) 52×25
    (d) 25×48 (e) 25×32 (f) 25×64

Exercise 4, pages 27 - 28

1. Add.
   (a) 499 + 307   (b) 201 + 359   (c) 599 + 742
   (d) 235 + 470   (e) 627 + 280   (f) 363 + 507

2. Subtract.
   (a) 732 − 99   (b) 443 − 299   (c) 522 − 60
   (d) 685 − 340   (e) 500 − 73   (f) 700 − 80

Multiply.
3. (a) 26 × 4   (b) 58 × 30   (c) 47 × 51
   (d) 35 × 6   (e) 82 × 40   (f) 61 × 61
   (g) 51 × 9   (h) 34 × 50   (i) 91 × 11

4. (a) 34 × 99   (b) 56 × 99   (c) 68 × 99
   (d) 16 × 25   (e) 44 × 25   (f) 72 × 25
   (g) 45 × 19   (h) 32 × 49   (i) 65 × 29

5. Angie earned $799 in the first month. In the second month, she earned $287 more than in the first month. How much did she earn in the second month?

6. A group of students was divided into 21 teams. There were 28 students in each team. How many students were there in the group?

7. Mr. Wilson bought a refrigerator at a sale. He paid the cashier $1000 and received $199 change. How much did the refrigerator cost?

8. There were 36 students in a class. Each student sold 25 tickets for a school fair. How many tickets were sold by the class?

9. Roger bought 6 dining chairs at $99 each. How much did he pay for the chairs together?

Word Problems

Alicia bought 420 mangoes for $378. She packed the mangoes in bags of 4 mangoes each and sold all the mangoes at $6 per bag. How much money did she earn?

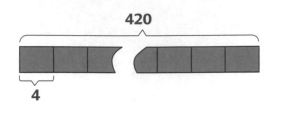

4 mangoes in 1 bag.

420 mangoes in ▢ bags.

$420 \div 4 = 105$

There were 105 bags of mangoes.

1 bag for $6.

105 bags for $ ▢ .

$6 \times 105 = \$630$

Alicia sold the mangoes for $630.

Amount mangoes were sold for – Original cost of mangoes = ▢

$\$630 - \$378 = \$$ ▢

Alicia earned $ ▢ .

1. Ryan and Juan shared $410 between them. Ryan received $100 more than Juan. How much money did Juan receive?

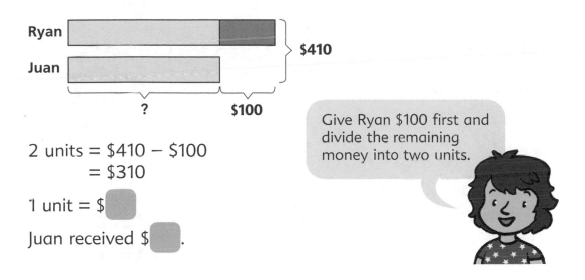

Give Ryan $100 first and divide the remaining money into two units.

2 units = $410 − $100
        = $310

1 unit = $⬚

Juan received $⬚.

2. Mary bought 3 dresses. Each dress cost the same amount. She gave the cashier $100 and got $16 change. How much did each dress cost?

3 units = $100 − $16

     = ⬚

1 unit = $⬚

Each dress cost $⬚.

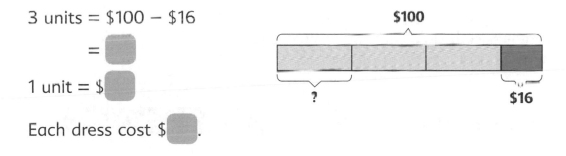

3. Peter collected a total of 1170 stamps. He collected 4 times as many U.S. stamps as foreign stamps. How many U.S. stamps did he collect?

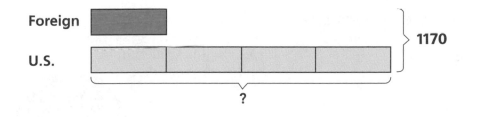

Exercise 5, pages 29 - 31

4. Mr. Given bought 2 similar T-shirts and a belt. He paid $50 to the cashier and received $3 change. If the belt cost $29, find the cost of each T-shirt.

$50 − $3 = $47

Mr. Given spent $47.

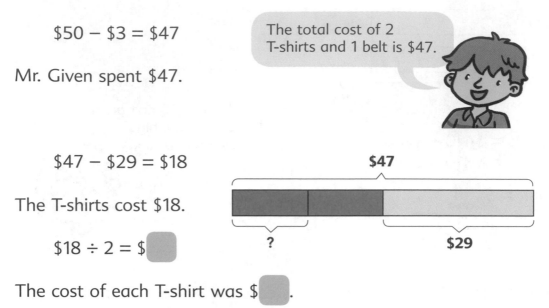

The total cost of 2 T-shirts and 1 belt is $47.

$47 − $29 = $18

The T-shirts cost $18.

$18 ÷ 2 = $⬚

The cost of each T-shirt was $⬚.

$47

?　　　　　　　　**$29**

5. Henry bought a compact disc and 3 similar videotapes. The compact disc cost $16. If a compact disc cost twice as much as a videotape, how much did he spend altogether?

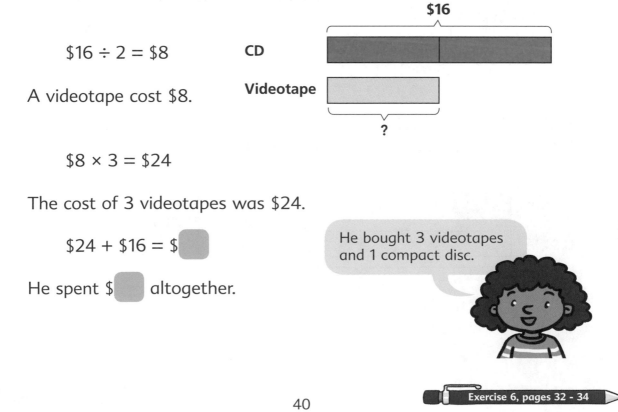

$16

CD

$16 ÷ 2 = $8

A videotape cost $8.

Videotape

?

$8 × 3 = $24

The cost of 3 videotapes was $24.

$24 + $16 = $⬚

He spent $⬚ altogether.

He bought 3 videotapes and 1 compact disc.

40

Exercise 6, pages 32 - 34

1. John is 15 kg heavier than Peter. Their total weight is 127 kg. Find John's weight.

2. There are 3 times as many boys as girls. If there are 24 more boys than girls, how many children are there altogether?

3. The total weight of Peter, David and Henry is 123 kg. Peter is 15 kg heavier than David. David is 3 kg lighter than Henry. Find Henry's weight.

4. Pablo has $180 and Ryan has $150. How much money must Pablo give Ryan so that they each will have an equal amount of money?

5. Matthew has twice as many stickers as David. How many stickers must Matthew give David so that they each will have 120 stickers?

6. Peter has twice as many stickers as Joe. Joe has 40 more stickers than Emily. They have 300 stickers altogether. How many stickers does Peter have?

7. At a book fair, Joe bought 24 books at 3 for $5 and had $2 left. How much money did he have at first?

8. Ryan bought 3 similar books and a magazine. He paid $30 to the cashier and received $5 change. If the magazine cost twice as much as each book, find the cost of the magazine.

9. Harry bought 155 oranges for $35. He found that 15 of them were rotten. He sold all the remaining oranges at 7 for $2. How much money did he earn?

10. John and Paul spent $45 altogether. John and Henry spent $65 altogether. If Henry spent 3 times as much as Paul, how much did John spend?

4 Multiplication by a 2-Digit Whole Number

(a) Multiply 78 by 30.

$$78 \times 30 = \boxed{}$$

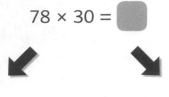

Method 1:

$$78 \times 30 = 78 \times 3 \times 10$$
$$= 234 \times 10$$
$$= 2340$$

Method 2:

$$\begin{array}{r} 78 \\ \times \quad 30 \\ \hline 2340 \end{array}$$

Multiply 78 by 3 first.

$$\begin{array}{r} 78 \\ \times \quad 3 \\ \hline 234 \end{array}$$

(b) Multiply 650 by 40.

$$\begin{array}{r} 650 \\ \times \quad 40 \\ \hline 26000 \end{array}$$

Multiply.

1. (a)
    $$\begin{array}{r} 5\,3 \\ \times\ \ 6\,0 \\ \hline \end{array}$$

    (b)
    $$\begin{array}{r} 2\,4\,7 \\ \times\ \ \ 8\,0 \\ \hline \end{array}$$

2. (a) 58 × 80   (b) 46 × 50   (c) 27 × 90
    (d) 207 × 60   (e) 739 × 40   (f) 641 × 70

3. (a)
    $$\begin{array}{r} 2\,4 \\ \times\ \ \ 1\,3 \\ \hline 7\,2 \leftarrow 24 \times 3 \\ 2\,4\,0 \leftarrow 24 \times 10 \\ \hline 3\,1\,2 \end{array}$$

    (b)
    $$\begin{array}{r} 5\,2 \\ \times\ \ \ 4\,7 \\ \hline \end{array}$$

    (c)
    $$\begin{array}{r} 3\,2\,5 \\ \times\ \ \ \ 5\,4 \\ \hline 1\,3\,0\,0 \leftarrow 325 \times 4 \\ 1\,6\,2\,5\,0 \leftarrow 325 \times 50 \\ \hline \end{array}$$

    (d)
    $$\begin{array}{r} 6\,1\,8 \\ \times\ \ \ \ 7\,2 \\ \hline \end{array}$$

4. (a) 67 × 44   (b) 53 × 48   (c) 29 × 96
    (d) 236 × 82   (e) 457 × 35   (f) 606 × 47

5. (a)
    $$\begin{array}{r} 4\,6\,3\,5 \\ \times\ \ \ \ \ 2\,6 \\ \hline \end{array}$$

    (b)
    $$\begin{array}{r} 8\,2\,4\,7 \\ \times\ \ \ \ \ 3\,8 \\ \hline \end{array}$$

6. (a) 3059 × 53   (b) 7105 × 62   (c) 2537 × 48
    (d) 3860 × 69   (e) 6394 × 57   (f) 5482 × 74

Exercise 7, pages 35 - 36

5 Division by a 2-Digit Whole Number

(a) Divide 140 by 20.

Method 1:

$$140 \div 20 = 7$$

140 ÷ 20

Method 2:

```
        7
20 ) 1 4 0
     1 4 0
         0
```

7 × 20 = 140

(b) Divide 150 by 20.

```
        7
20 ) 1 5 0
     1 4 0
       1 0
```

150 ÷ 20
I cannot divide 15 by 2 exactly.
So I use method 2.

44

1. Divide.

   (a)
   $$30 \overline{)70}$$

   (b)
   $$60 \overline{)430}$$

   (c)
   $$20 \overline{)89}$$

   (d)
   $$70 \overline{)625}$$

2. Divide.

   (a) $90 \div 50$ (b) $79 \div 40$ (c) $85 \div 30$
   (d) $540 \div 70$ (e) $613 \div 90$ (f) $438 \div 60$

3. Divide 74 by 21.

   $$\begin{array}{r} 3 \\ 21 \overline{)74} \\ \underline{63} \\ 11 \end{array}$$

   $$\begin{array}{r} 3 \\ 20 \overline{)74} \end{array}$$
   The estimated quotient is 3.

4. Divide 256 by 47.

   $$\begin{array}{r} 5 \\ 47 \overline{)256} \\ \underline{235} \\ 21 \end{array}$$

   $$\begin{array}{r} 5 \\ 50 \overline{)256} \end{array}$$
   The estimated quotient is 5.

5. Divide.

   (a) $63 \div 17$ (b) $48 \div 23$ (c) $85 \div 38$
   (d) $76 \div 34$ (e) $94 \div 43$ (f) $57 \div 29$
   (g) $149 \div 67$ (h) $509 \div 84$ (i) $756 \div 95$
   (j) $668 \div 72$ (k) $279 \div 56$ (l) $183 \div 44$

   Exercise 8, page 37

6. Divide 89 by 24.

   $$\begin{array}{r} 4 \\ 20 \overline{)89} \end{array}$$
   The estimated quotient is 4.

   $$\begin{array}{r} 4 \\ 24 \overline{)89} \\ \underline{96} \end{array} \quad \Rightarrow \quad \begin{array}{r} 3 \\ 24 \overline{)89} \\ \underline{72} \\ 17 \end{array}$$

   The estimated quotient 4
   is too big. Try 3.

45

7. Divide 78 by 26.

$$30\overline{)78} \quad \mathbf{2}$$

The estimated quotient is 2.

$$26\overline{)78} \quad \begin{array}{r}\mathbf{2}\\78\\-52\\\hline 26\end{array}$$

$$26\overline{)78} \quad \begin{array}{r}\mathbf{3}\\78\\-78\\\hline 0\end{array}$$

The estimated quotient 2 is too small. Try 3.

8. Divide.
   (a) 68 ÷ 17
   (b) 77 ÷ 25
   (c) 94 ÷ 33
   (d) 83 ÷ 21
   (e) 84 ÷ 43
   (f) 75 ÷ 15

9. Divide 285 by 33.

$$30\overline{)285} \quad \mathbf{9}$$

The estimated quotient is 9.

$$33\overline{)285} \quad \begin{array}{r}\mathbf{9}\\285\\297\end{array}$$

$$33\overline{)285} \quad \begin{array}{r}\mathbf{8}\\285\\-264\\\hline 21\end{array}$$

The estimated quotient 9 is too big. Try 8.

10. Divide 473 by 78.

$$80\overline{)473} \quad \mathbf{5}$$

The estimated quotient is 5.

$$78\overline{)473} \quad \begin{array}{r}\mathbf{5}\\473\\-390\\\hline 83\end{array}$$

$$78\overline{)473} \quad \begin{array}{r}\mathbf{6}\\473\\-468\\\hline 5\end{array}$$

The estimated quotient 5 is too small. Try 6.

11. Divide.
   (a) 207 ÷ 23
   (b) 236 ÷ 39
   (c) 474 ÷ 79
   (d) 572 ÷ 64
   (e) 464 ÷ 58
   (f) 640 ÷ 93

Exercise 9, page 38

12. Divide 570 by 16.

Divide 57 tens by 16.

```
       3
16 ) 5 7 0
     4 8
       9
```

Divide 90 by 16.

```
      3 5
16 ) 5 7 0
     4 8
     9 0
     8 0
     1 0
```

13. Divide.

(a)
```
        2 5
34 ) 8 7 0
     6 8
     1 9 0
     1 7 0
       2 0
```

(b)
```
        3 0
28 ) 8 6 2
     8 4
       2 2
```

(c)
```
47 ) 7 0 3
```

(d)
```
15 ) 6 1 2
```

14. Divide.
   (a) 552 ÷ 24
   (d) 399 ÷ 31
   (b) 660 ÷ 29
   (e) 708 ÷ 67
   (c) 925 ÷ 46
   (f) 374 ÷ 18

Exercise 10, page 39

15. Divide.

(a)
```
         2 3 4
28 ) 6 5 5 2
     5 6
       9 5
       8 4
       1 1 2
       1 1 2
             0
```

(b)
```
          8 3
52 ) 4 3 2 8
     4 1 6
       1 6 8
       1 5 6
           1 2
```

(c)
```
64 ) 6 8 2 0
```

(d)
```
45 ) 3 1 8 5
```

16. Divide.
   (a) 6692 ÷ 28
   (d) 6008 ÷ 56
   (b) 2409 ÷ 18
   (e) 1054 ÷ 37
   (c) 1495 ÷ 45
   (f) 9864 ÷ 29

Exercise 11, page 40

Multiply.

	(a)	(b)	(c)
1.	407 × 84	690 × 49	941 × 73
2.	5395 × 51	7404 × 85	3092 × 63

Divide.

	(a)	(b)	(c)
3.	89 ÷ 24	92 ÷ 33	56 ÷ 18
4.	848 ÷ 16	403 ÷ 67	505 ÷ 53
5.	722 ÷ 38	895 ÷ 23	999 ÷ 42
6.	7684 ÷ 78	1340 ÷ 23	9670 ÷ 54

7. A cook uses 12 cups of water to make a pot of soup. How many cups of water does he need if he wants to make 36 pots of soup?

8. Mr. Hill has to drive to a city which is 240 km from Portland. If his car can travel 15 km on 1 liter of gas, how many liters of gas does he need for the trip?

9. 1064 balloons were shared equally among 38 students. How many balloons did each student receive?

10. Mrs. Garcia sold 96 figurines at a garage sale. The figurines were sold in boxes of 12. She sold all the figurines at $7 per box. How much money did she receive?

11. Mr. Kent buys a car and pays by installments. Each installment is $827. If he still has to pay $280 after paying 72 installments, how much does the car cost?

12. Miss Lee sold 2034 concert tickets at $16 per ticket. She also sold 840 programs at $3 each. How much money did she collect altogether?

13. 70 students were divided into 14 teams. In each team there were 2 girls. How many boys were there altogether?

14. Mrs. Ward bought 840 eggs. She sold them in trays of 12 eggs each. How much money did she receive if the selling price per tray was $3?

1. (a) What number is one thousand less than one million?
   (b) What number is one hundred thousand less than one hundred million?

2. Find the value of each of the following expressions.
   (a) $12 \div (6 - 2) + 7 \times 2 - 8$ (b) $20 - 8 \div 2 \times 4 + 1$
   (c) $6 \times (5 + 6) - 18 + 8$ (d) $(7 - 3) \times 3 + 9 \div 3$

3. $51{,}283{,}000 = \boxed{} + 80{,}000 + 3000$

4. What is the greatest whole number that will make the statements true?

   (a) $75 + \boxed{} < 100$ (b) $\boxed{} - 97 < 100$

5. What is the smallest number that can be formed from the digits 7, 9, 0, 2, 6, and 5?

6. Mimi left home at 8:25 a.m. She returned home at 4:15 p.m. How long was she away from home?

7. What is the missing number in each $\boxed{}$?
   (a) $36 \times 25 = 9 \times \boxed{}$ (b) $7 \times 45 = 21 \times \boxed{}$

   (c) $25 \times 24 = 100 \times \boxed{}$ (d) $15 \times 18 = 3 \times \boxed{}$

   (e) $8 + 8 + 6 \times 2 = \boxed{} \times 6 + 28$ (f) $46 \times 7 = (40 \times \boxed{}) + (6 \times \boxed{})$

8. Multiply.
   (a) 62×99 (b) 84×29 (c) 76×25

9. Add or subtract.
   (a) $698 + 83$ (b) $943 - 499$ (c) $1248 + 399$

10. Multiply.
    (a) 71×29 (b) 86×36 (c) 35×94
    (d) 258×24 (e) 574×62 (f) 392×44
    (g) 7067×39 (h) 6830×72 (i) 4872×44

11. Divide.
    (a) 76 ÷ 23   (b) 95 ÷ 64   (c) 81 ÷ 38
    (d) 510 ÷ 67   (e) 337 ÷ 72   (f) 409 ÷ 53
    (g) 3640 ÷ 57   (h) 5509 ÷ 63   (i) 8513 ÷ 36

12. Write the prime factorization of 48 using exponents.

13. David is 18 lb lighter than Pablo. Their total weight is 250 lb. Find David's weight.

14. A number when divided by 32 has a quotient of 8 with 3 as the remainder. Find the number.

15. Aaron saved twice as much as Roger. Maria saved $60 more than Roger. If they saved $600 altogether, how much did Maria save?

16. Paul picked 357 oranges the first day and 497 oranges the next day. He packed the oranges in bags of 12.
    (a) How many oranges did he have left over?
    (b) If he sold each bag of oranges for $2, how much money did he receive?

17. Mr. Dunlap bought 40 boxes of grapefruit for $258. There were 24 grapefruits in each box. He threw away 15 rotten grapefruits and sold the rest at 3 for $1. How much money did he earn?

18. Peter put 1827 books equally on 43 shelves.
    (a) How many books were there on each shelf?
    (b) How many books were left over?

19. A man had 15 crates of oranges. Each crate had the same number of oranges. He sold 70 oranges on Monday and twice as many oranges on Tuesday. He had 90 oranges left. How many oranges were there in each crate at first?

20. A bakery sold 328 cakes on Monday. It sold 178 more cakes on Monday than on Tuesday. Each cake was sold for $19. How much money did the bakery receive from selling the cakes?

50

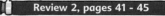 Review 2, pages 41 - 45

3 FRACTIONS

① Comparing Fractions

Which is greater, $\frac{2}{5}$ or $\frac{3}{8}$?

I use fraction discs to compare the fractions.

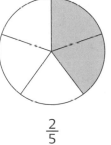

$\frac{2}{5}$

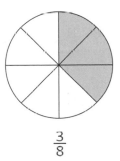

$\frac{3}{8}$

In the fraction $\frac{2}{5}$, 2 is the **numerator** and 5 is the **denominator**.

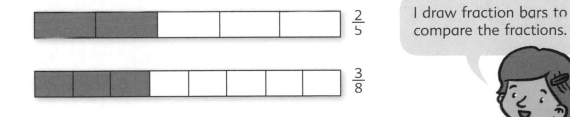

$\frac{2}{5}$

$\frac{3}{8}$

I draw fraction bars to compare the fractions.

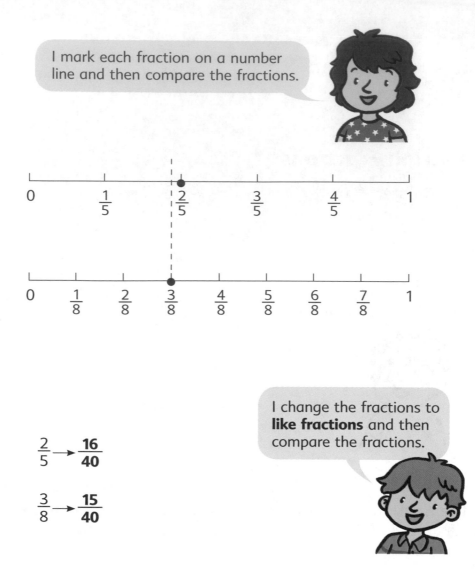

I mark each fraction on a number line and then compare the fractions.

I change the fractions to **like fractions** and then compare the fractions.

$$\frac{2}{5} \rightarrow \frac{16}{40}$$

$$\frac{3}{8} \rightarrow \frac{15}{40}$$

Like fractions are fractions with common denominators. It is easy to compare like fractions. Why?

1. There are 12 flowers. 8 of them are roses. What fraction of the flowers are roses?

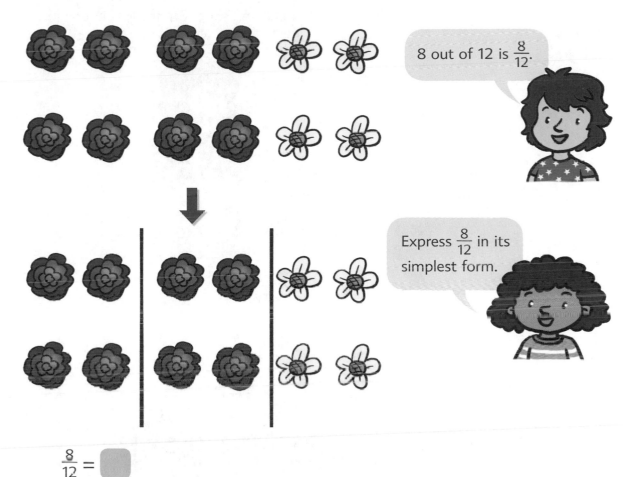

8 out of 12 is $\frac{8}{12}$.

Express $\frac{8}{12}$ in its simplest form.

$\frac{8}{12} =$

of the flowers are roses.

2. Write each of the following fractions in its simplest form.

(a) $\frac{8}{12}$ (b) $\frac{9}{12}$ (c) $\frac{6}{9}$ (d) $\frac{6}{12}$

3. Write >, < or = in each ⬤.

(a) $\frac{3}{2}$ ⬤ $\frac{5}{4}$ (b) $2\frac{1}{2}$ ⬤ $2\frac{1}{7}$ (c) $3\frac{8}{9}$ ⬤ 4

(d) $1\frac{5}{6}$ ⬤ $\frac{11}{6}$ (e) $4\frac{2}{3}$ ⬤ $\frac{9}{2}$ (f) 3 ⬤ $\frac{15}{4}$

Exercise 1, pages 46 – 49

② Fractions and Division

4 children share 3 pancakes equally.
Each child receives 3 quarters.

$$3 \div 4 = \frac{3}{4}$$

4 children share 5 pancakes equally.
Each child receives 5 quarters.

$$5 \div 4 = \frac{5}{4}$$

Here is another way to show that $5 \div 4 = \frac{5}{4}$.

$$4 \overline{)\,5} \\ \underline{4} \\ 1$$ (quotient 1)

Each child receives 1 pancake first. Share the remaining pancake.

$$1 \div 4 = \frac{1}{4}$$

Each child receives 1 and $\frac{1}{4}$ pancakes.

An **improper fraction** has a value equal to, or greater than one. The numerator is equal to, or greater than the denominator.

$$5 \div 4 = 1\frac{1}{4}$$
$$= \frac{4}{4} + \frac{1}{4}$$
$$= \frac{5}{4}$$

1. Express $\frac{11}{4}$ as a mixed number.

Method 1:

$$\frac{11}{4} = \frac{8}{4} + \frac{3}{4}$$
$$= 2\frac{3}{4}$$

A **mixed number** is made up of a whole number and a fraction.

Method 2:

$$\frac{11}{4} = 11 \div 4 = \boxed{}$$

$$4 \overline{)\,1\,1} \quad (2) \\ \underline{8} \\ 3$$

55

2. A bucket contains 8 qt of water. If the water is poured equally into 3 jugs, how much water is there in each jug?

$$8 \div 3 = \boxed{}$$

$$\begin{array}{r} 2 \\ 3\overline{)8} \\ \underline{6} \\ 2 \end{array}$$

There are qt of water in each jug.

3. Find the value of $22 \div 8$.

Method 1:

$$22 \div 8 = 2\frac{6}{8}$$

$$= 2\,\frac{\boxed{}}{4}$$

$$\begin{array}{r} 2 \\ 8\overline{)22} \\ \underline{16} \\ 6 \end{array}$$

Method 2:

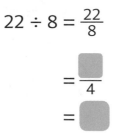

$$22 \div 8 = \frac{22}{8}$$

$$= \frac{\boxed{}}{4}$$

$$= \boxed{}$$

4. Find the value of
   (a) $7 \div 3$ (b) $14 \div 5$ (c) $21 \div 6$ (d) $77 \div 9$

 Exercise 2, pages 50 - 51

PRACTICE A

1. Express each of the following as a whole number or a mixed number in its simplest form.

   (a) $\frac{13}{5}$

   (b) $\frac{21}{3}$

   (c) $\frac{24}{9}$

   (d) $\frac{50}{6}$

2. Express each of the following answers as a mixed number in its simplest form.
   (a) $30 \div 8$
   (b) $21 \div 4$
   (c) $35 \div 10$
   (d) $78 \div 7$

3. Nancy cut a ribbon into 8 equal pieces. If the ribbon was 26 m long, how many meters long was each piece?

4. Mrs. York bought 3 m of cloth. She used the cloth to make 9 pillow cases of the same size. How much cloth in meters did she use for each pillow case?

5. Mary baked 10 cakes of the same size. She divided the cakes into 4 equal shares. How many cakes were there in each share?

6. Peter poured 2 liters of milk equally into 5 jugs. How much milk was there in each jug?

7. A red ribbon 11 m long is 5 times as long as a blue ribbon. How long is the blue ribbon?

8. A packet of flour weighing 4 kg was divided into 6 equal shares. What was the weight of each share in kilograms?

3 Addition and Subtraction of Unlike Fractions

1. Add $\frac{3}{8}$ and $\frac{1}{6}$.

$$\frac{3}{8} + \frac{1}{6} = \frac{\boxed{}}{24} + \frac{\boxed{}}{24}$$

$$= \frac{\boxed{}}{24}$$

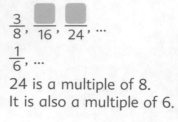

$\frac{3}{8}, \frac{\boxed{}}{16}, \frac{\boxed{}}{24}, \cdots$

$\frac{1}{6}, \cdots$

24 is a multiple of 8.
It is also a multiple of 6.

2. Add $\frac{2}{3}$ and $\frac{2}{5}$.

$$\frac{2}{3} + \frac{2}{5} = \frac{\boxed{}}{15} + \frac{\boxed{}}{15}$$

$$= \frac{\boxed{}}{15}$$

$$= \boxed{}$$

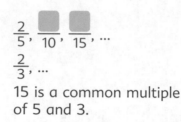

$\frac{2}{5}, \frac{\boxed{}}{10}, \frac{\boxed{}}{15}, \cdots$

$\frac{2}{3}, \cdots$

15 is a common multiple of 5 and 3.

3. Add $\frac{7}{10}$ and $\frac{5}{6}$.

$$\frac{7}{10} + \frac{5}{6} = \frac{\boxed{}}{30} + \frac{\boxed{}}{30}$$

$$= \frac{\boxed{}}{30}$$

$$= \frac{\boxed{}}{15}$$

$$= \boxed{}$$

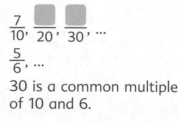

$\frac{7}{10}, \frac{\boxed{}}{20}, \frac{\boxed{}}{30}, \cdots$

$\frac{5}{6}, \cdots$

30 is a common multiple of 10 and 6.

4. Add. Give each answer in its simplest form.

(a) $\frac{7}{9} + \frac{5}{6}$

(b) $\frac{3}{4} + \frac{5}{12}$

(c) $\frac{3}{10} + \frac{5}{6}$

Exercise 3, pages 52 - 53

5. Subtract $\frac{1}{6}$ from $\frac{7}{8}$.

$$\frac{7}{8} - \frac{1}{6} = \frac{\boxed{}}{24} - \frac{\boxed{}}{24}$$

$$= \frac{\boxed{}}{24}$$

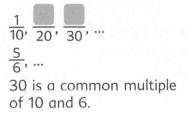

$\frac{7}{8}, \frac{\boxed{}}{16}, \frac{\boxed{}}{24}, \cdots$

$\frac{1}{6}, \cdots$

24 is a common multiple of 8 and 6.

6. Subtract $\frac{1}{10}$ from $\frac{5}{6}$.

$$\frac{5}{6} - \frac{1}{10} = \frac{\boxed{}}{30} - \frac{\boxed{}}{30}$$

$$= \frac{\boxed{}}{30}$$

$$= \frac{\boxed{}}{15}$$

$\frac{1}{10}, \frac{\boxed{}}{20}, \frac{\boxed{}}{30}, \cdots$

$\frac{5}{6}, \cdots$

30 is a common multiple of 10 and 6.

7. Subtract $\frac{5}{6}$ from $1\frac{7}{10}$.

$$1\frac{7}{10} - \frac{5}{6} = \frac{\boxed{}}{30} - \frac{\boxed{}}{30}$$

$$= \frac{\boxed{}}{30} - \frac{\boxed{}}{30}$$

$$= \frac{\boxed{}}{15}$$

$\frac{7}{10}, \frac{\boxed{}}{20}, \frac{\boxed{}}{30}, \cdots$

$\frac{5}{6}, \cdots$

30 is a common multiple of 10 and 6.

8. Subtract. Give each answer in its simplest form.

(a) $\frac{5}{6} - \frac{3}{10}$

(b) $1\frac{2}{3} - \frac{11}{12}$

(c) $1\frac{1}{10} - \frac{5}{6}$

Exercise 4, pages 54 - 55

Add or subtract. Give each answer in its simplest form.

	(a)	(b)	(c)
1.	$\frac{7}{12} + \frac{5}{6}$	$\frac{9}{10} + \frac{1}{6}$	$\frac{5}{6} + \frac{7}{8}$
2.	$\frac{2}{3} - \frac{5}{12}$	$\frac{5}{6} - \frac{7}{10}$	$\frac{3}{4} - \frac{1}{6}$
3.	$\frac{1}{6} + \frac{3}{10}$	$\frac{2}{3} + \frac{1}{12}$	$\frac{5}{12} + \frac{1}{8}$
4.	$1\frac{3}{8} - \frac{7}{12}$	$1\frac{1}{3} - \frac{7}{10}$	$1\frac{3}{10} - \frac{5}{6}$

5. John mowed $\frac{2}{5}$ of a lawn. His brother mowed another $\frac{1}{4}$ of it. What fraction of the lawn did they mow?

6. Samy took $\frac{3}{4}$ hour to travel from home to the zoo. He took $1\frac{1}{4}$ hours to return home. How much longer did he take to return home than to go to the zoo?

7. Mary ate $\frac{1}{8}$ of a cake. Peter ate another $\frac{1}{4}$ of it.
   (a) What fraction of the cake did they eat altogether?
   (b) What fraction of the cake did Peter eat more than Mary?

8. Ali went to a bookshop. He spent $\frac{3}{5}$ of of his money on books and $\frac{1}{4}$ of it on a pen.

   (a) What fraction of his money did he spend altogether?
   (b) What fraction of his money did he have left?

4 Addition and Subtraction of Mixed Numbers

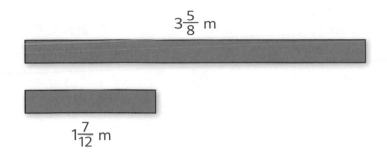

$3\frac{5}{8}$ m

$1\frac{7}{12}$ m

(a) Find the total length of $3\frac{5}{8}$ m and $1\frac{7}{12}$ m.

$$3\frac{5}{8} + 1\frac{7}{12} = 4\frac{5}{8} + \frac{7}{12}$$

$$= 4\frac{15}{24} + \frac{14}{24}$$

$$3\frac{5}{8} \xrightarrow{+1} \boxed{} \xrightarrow{+\frac{7}{12}} \boxed{}$$

$$= 4\,\frac{\boxed{}}{24}$$

$$= \boxed{}$$

The total length is $\boxed{}$ m.

(b) Add $4\frac{7}{12}$ and $1\frac{3}{4}$.

$$4\frac{7}{12} + 1\frac{3}{4} = 5\frac{7}{12} + \frac{3}{4}$$

$$= 5\frac{7}{12} + \frac{9}{12}$$

Express the answer in its simplest form.

$$= 5\,\frac{\boxed{}}{12}$$

$$= 5\,\frac{\boxed{}}{3}$$

$$= \boxed{}$$

1. Add $3\frac{1}{6}$ and $1\frac{9}{10}$.

$$3\frac{1}{6} + 1\frac{9}{10} = 4\frac{1}{6} + \frac{9}{10}$$

$$= 4\frac{\boxed{}}{30} + \frac{\boxed{}}{30}$$

$$= 4\frac{\boxed{}}{30}$$

$$= \boxed{}$$

Exercise 5, pages 56 - 57

2. Find the difference in length between $4\frac{3}{4}$ m and $3\frac{7}{12}$ m.

$$4\frac{3}{4} - 3\frac{7}{12} = 1\frac{3}{4} - \frac{7}{12}$$

$$= 1\frac{9}{12} - \frac{7}{12}$$

$$= 1\frac{\boxed{}}{12}$$

$$= \boxed{}$$

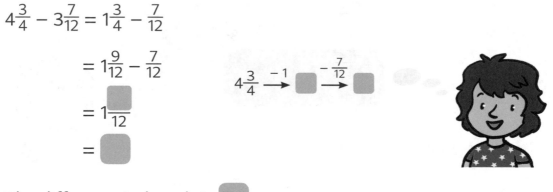

$4\frac{3}{4} \xrightarrow{-1} \boxed{} \xrightarrow{-\frac{7}{12}} \boxed{}$

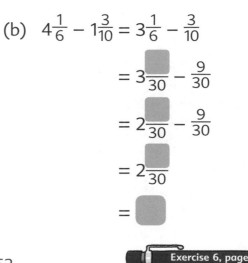

The difference in length is $\boxed{}$ m.

3. Subtract.

(a) $3\frac{1}{6} - 1\frac{5}{9} = 2\frac{1}{6} - \frac{5}{9}$

$$= 2\frac{3}{18} - \frac{10}{18}$$

$$= 1\frac{\boxed{}}{18} - \frac{10}{18}$$

$$= \boxed{}$$

(b) $4\frac{1}{6} - 1\frac{3}{10} = 3\frac{1}{6} - \frac{3}{10}$

$$= 3\frac{\boxed{}}{30} - \frac{9}{30}$$

$$= 2\frac{\boxed{}}{30} - \frac{9}{30}$$

$$= 2\frac{\boxed{}}{30}$$

$$= \boxed{}$$

Exercise 6, pages 58 - 59

PRACTICE C

Add or subtract. Give each answer in its simplest form.

	(a)	(b)	(c)
1.	$2\frac{2}{3} + 1\frac{5}{9}$	$2\frac{1}{8} + 1\frac{5}{6}$	$1\frac{1}{4} + 2\frac{5}{6}$
2.	$3\frac{5}{6} - 1\frac{1}{3}$	$3\frac{4}{5} - 1\frac{3}{10}$	$4\frac{5}{6} - 1\frac{1}{4}$
3.	$3\frac{2}{9} + 1\frac{1}{6}$	$2\frac{5}{6} + 5\frac{1}{2}$	$2\frac{5}{6} + 1\frac{3}{8}$
4.	$4\frac{1}{6} - 1\frac{2}{3}$	$3\frac{1}{6} - 2\frac{1}{10}$	$3\frac{3}{10} - 1\frac{1}{6}$

5. Robert jogged $1\frac{2}{5}$ km. His brother jogged $2\frac{1}{2}$ km. Who jogged the longer distance? How much longer?

6. There were $3\frac{1}{6}$ loaves of bread on the table. After breakfast, there were $1\frac{2}{3}$ loaves left. How many loaves of bread were eaten?

7. A container has a capacity of 3 liters. It contains $1\frac{3}{4}$ liters of water. How much more water is needed to fill the container completely?

8. Ann planned to spend $1\frac{1}{2}$ hours to cook a meal. She finished the cooking in $1\frac{1}{12}$ hours instead. How much earlier did she finish the cooking?

9. The total length of two ribbons is $2\frac{3}{4}$ m. If one ribbon is $1\frac{1}{3}$ m long, what is the length of the other ribbon?

5 Multiplying a Fraction and a Whole Number

Sam drinks $\frac{1}{2}$ a liter of milk a day.
How many liters of milk will he drink in 5 days?

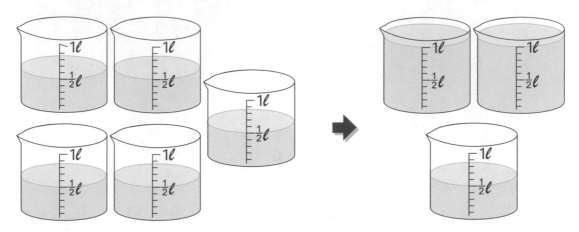

$$\frac{1}{2} \times 5 = \frac{5}{2}$$
$$= 2\frac{1}{2}$$

$$\frac{1}{2} + \frac{1}{2} + \frac{1}{2} + \frac{1}{2} + \frac{1}{2} = \frac{5}{2}$$

He will drink $2\frac{1}{2}$ liters of milk in 5 days.

$$\frac{1}{2} \times 5 = \frac{1 \times 5}{2}$$

1. Multiply $\frac{1}{2}$ by 8.

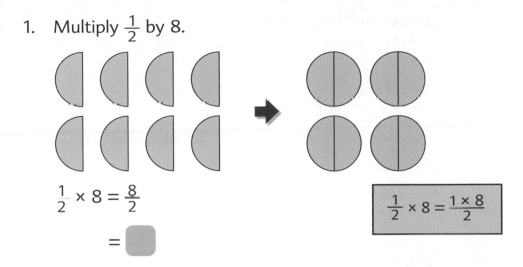

$\frac{1}{2} \times 8 = \frac{8}{2}$

$= $

$$\frac{1}{2} \times 8 = \frac{1 \times 8}{2}$$

2. Multiply $\frac{1}{4}$ by 6.

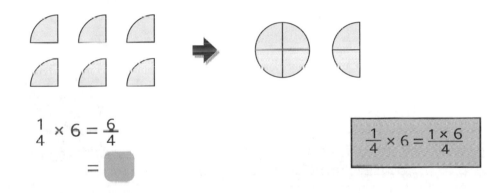

$\frac{1}{4} \times 6 = \frac{6}{4}$

$= $

$$\frac{1}{4} \times 6 = \frac{1 \times 6}{4}$$

3. Multiply $\frac{2}{3}$ by 4.

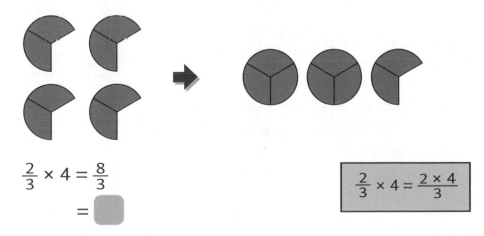

$\frac{2}{3} \times 4 = \frac{8}{3}$

$= $

$$\frac{2}{3} \times 4 = \frac{2 \times 4}{3}$$

4. Multiply. Give each answer in its simplest form.

   (a) $\frac{1}{5} \times 3$ (b) $\frac{1}{3} \times 6$ (c) $\frac{1}{6} \times 8$

   (d) $\frac{3}{8} \times 4$ (e) $\frac{7}{10} \times 5$ (f) $\frac{5}{12} \times 4$

Exercise 7, pages 60 - 61

5. Multiply 5 by $\frac{1}{2}$.

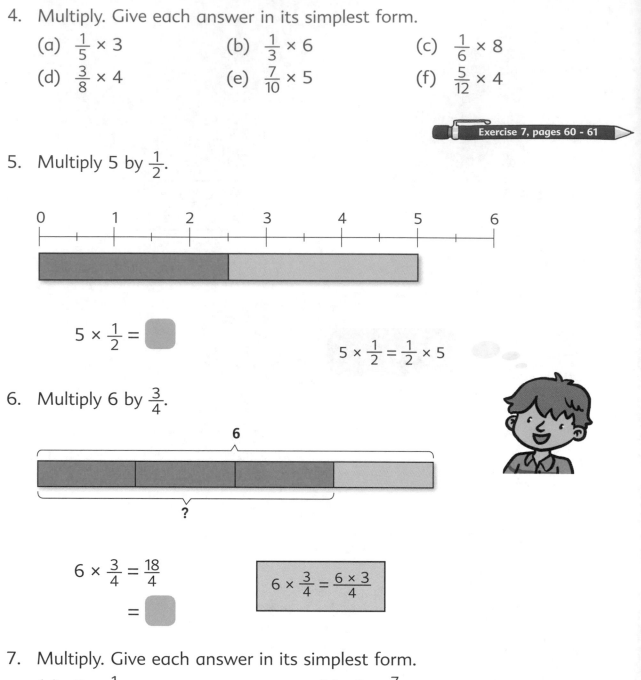

$$5 \times \frac{1}{2} = \boxed{}$$

$$5 \times \frac{1}{2} = \frac{1}{2} \times 5$$

6. Multiply 6 by $\frac{3}{4}$.

6

?

$$6 \times \frac{3}{4} = \frac{18}{4}$$
$$= \boxed{}$$

$$6 \times \frac{3}{4} = \frac{6 \times 3}{4}$$

7. Multiply. Give each answer in its simplest form.

   (a) $2 \times \frac{1}{5}$ (b) $3 \times \frac{7}{8}$

   (c) $3 \times \frac{2}{3}$ (d) $8 \times \frac{3}{4}$

   (e) $9 \times \frac{1}{6}$ (f) $12 \times \frac{3}{8}$

Exercise 8, pages 62 - 63

6 Fraction of a Set

Lihua bought 12 eggs. She used $\frac{2}{3}$ of them to bake a cake. How many eggs did she use?

Method 1:

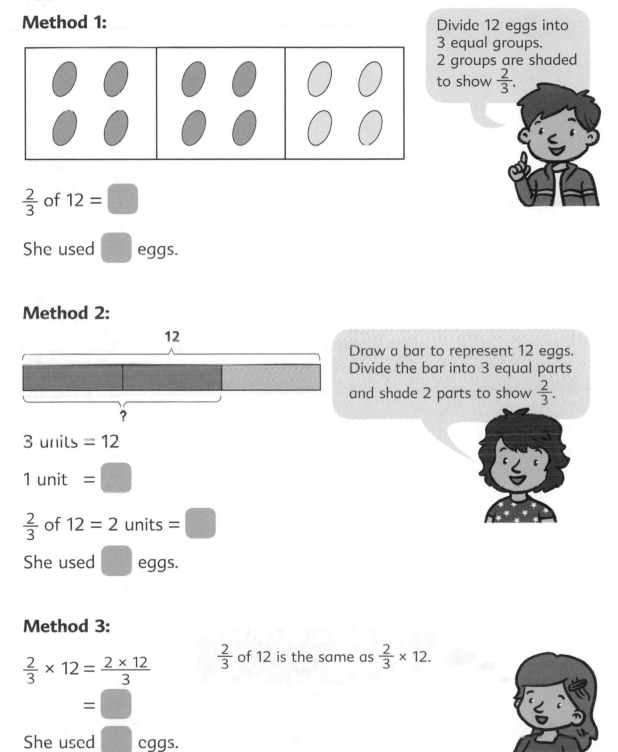

Divide 12 eggs into 3 equal groups. 2 groups are shaded to show $\frac{2}{3}$.

$\frac{2}{3}$ of 12 = ☐

She used ☐ eggs.

Method 2:

12

?

Draw a bar to represent 12 eggs. Divide the bar into 3 equal parts and shade 2 parts to show $\frac{2}{3}$.

3 units = 12

1 unit = ☐

$\frac{2}{3}$ of 12 = 2 units = ☐

She used ☐ eggs.

Method 3:

$\frac{2}{3} \times 12 = \frac{2 \times 12}{3}$

$= ☐$

$\frac{2}{3}$ of 12 is the same as $\frac{2}{3} \times 12$.

She used ☐ eggs.

1. Find the value of $\frac{1}{4}$ of 5.

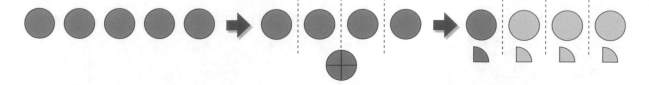

$\frac{1}{4}$ of 5 = $1\frac{1}{4}$

I divide 5 into 4 equal groups. First, one whole goes into each group. There is one whole leftover. I divide it into fourths and put one fourth into each group.

$\frac{1}{4}$ of 5 = $\frac{1}{4} \times 5$

$= \frac{1 \times 5}{4}$

$= \frac{5}{4}$

$= 1\frac{1}{4}$

I can also do it in another way. I divide each whole into fourths. There are 20 fourths. I can put 5 fourths into each group.

2. Find the value of $\frac{3}{4}$ of 5.

$\frac{3}{4}$ of 5 = $\frac{3}{4} \times 5$

$=$ ▢

3. Find the value of $\frac{3}{4}$ of 9.

$\frac{3}{4} \times 9 = \frac{3 \times 9}{4}$

$=$ ▢

4. (a) Find the value of $\frac{2}{3}$ of 5.

$$\frac{2}{3} \times 5 = \frac{2 \times 5}{3}$$
$$= \boxed{}$$

$$\frac{2}{3} \times 5 = 5 \times \frac{2}{3}$$

(b) Multiply 5 by $\frac{2}{3}$.

$$5 \times \frac{2}{3} = \frac{5 \times 2}{3}$$
$$= \boxed{}$$

5. Find the value of $\frac{3}{8} \times 20$.

Method 1:

$$\frac{3}{8} \times 20 = \frac{3 \times 20}{8}$$
$$= \frac{60}{8}$$
$$= \boxed{}$$

Write $\frac{60}{8}$ in its simplest form.

Method 2:

$$\frac{3}{8} \times 20 = \frac{3 \times \cancel{20}^{5}}{\cancel{8}_{2}}$$
$$= \frac{3 \times 5}{2}$$
$$= \boxed{}$$

4 is a common factor of 20 and 8.
Divide 20 and 8 by 4.

Method 3:

$$\frac{3}{\cancel{8}_{2}} \times \cancel{20}^{5} = \frac{3 \times 5}{2}$$
$$= \boxed{}$$

6. Multiply. Give each answer in its simplest form.
(a) $\frac{2}{5} \times 10$ (b) $\frac{5}{6} \times 8$ (c) $\frac{3}{4} \times 18$

(d) $12 \times \frac{3}{4}$ (e) $14 \times \frac{1}{6}$ (f) $20 \times \frac{3}{8}$

(g) $\frac{10}{3} \times 6$ (h) $\frac{12}{5} \times 25$ (i) $\frac{11}{4} \times 10$

(j) $15 \times \frac{7}{3}$ (k) $21 \times \frac{11}{9}$ (l) $16 \times \frac{13}{12}$

7. Find the value of
(a) $\frac{1}{4}$ of 80   (b) $\frac{1}{5}$ of 50

(c) $\frac{2}{3}$ of 90   (d) $\frac{1}{3} \times 300$

(e) $\frac{3}{4} \times 400$ (f) $\frac{2}{5} \times 100$

Exercise 9, pages 64 - 65

8. How many months are there in $\frac{5}{6}$ of a year?

$\frac{5}{6}$ of a year $= \frac{5}{6} \times 12$ months   1 year = 12 months

$= \boxed{}$ months

9. Express $\frac{3}{5}$ m in centimeters.

$\frac{3}{5}$ m $= \frac{3}{5} \times 100$ cm   1 m = 100 cm

$= \boxed{}$ cm

Conversion of Measurements

Length

1 m = 100 cm

1 km = 1000 m

1 yd = 3 ft

1 ft = 12 in.

1 mi = 5280 ft

Weight

1 kg = 1000 g

1 lb = 16 oz

Time

1 year = 12 months

1 week = 7 days

1 day = 24 hours

1 hour = 60 minutes

1 minute = 60 seconds

Volume of liquid/capacity

1 ℓ = 1000 ml

1 gal = 4 qt

1 qt = 2 pt

1 qt = 4 c

10. Find the missing number in each ▢.

   (a) $\frac{1}{2}$ min = ▢ s   (b) $\frac{7}{10}$ kg = ▢ g   (c) $\frac{2}{5}$ km = ▢ m

   (d) $\frac{3}{10}$ ℓ = ▢ ml   (e) $\frac{3}{4}$ year = ▢ months   (f) $\frac{1}{6}$ h = ▢ min

   (g) $\frac{2}{3}$ yd = ▢ ft   (h) $\frac{1}{4}$ lb = ▢ oz   (i) $\frac{3}{4}$ gal = ▢ qt

11. Express $2\frac{3}{4}$ h in hours and minutes.

   $\frac{3}{4}$ h = $\frac{3}{4}$ × 60 min = ▢ min

   $2\frac{3}{4}$ h = ▢ h ▢ min

12. Find the missing number in each ▢.

   (a) $2\frac{1}{3}$ h = ▢ h ▢ min   (b) $4\frac{2}{3}$ yd = ▢ yd ▢ ft

   (c) $5\frac{1}{4}$ gal = ▢ gal ▢ qt   (d) $3\frac{1}{2}$ km = ▢ km ▢ m

   (e) $14\frac{9}{10}$ ℓ = ▢ ℓ ▢ ml   (f) $6\frac{1}{4}$ years = ▢ years ▢ months

71

Exercise 10, pages 66 - 67

13. Express $3\frac{2}{5}$ km in meters.

3 km = 3000 m

$\frac{2}{5}$ km = $\frac{2}{5}$ × 1000 m

= 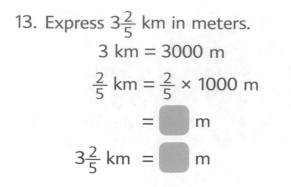 m

$3\frac{2}{5}$ km = ⬜ m

$3\frac{2}{5}$ km = 3 km + $\frac{2}{5}$ km

14. Express $2\frac{1}{4}$ days in hours.

2 days = ⬜ h

$\frac{1}{4}$ day = ⬜ h

$2\frac{1}{4}$ days = ⬜ h

15. Find the missing number in each ⬜.

(a) $2\frac{1}{2}$ m = ⬜ cm

(b) $1\frac{1}{2}$ lb = ⬜ oz

(c) $3\frac{1}{2}$ gal = ⬜ qt

(d) $2\frac{3}{4}$ years = ⬜ months

(e) $1\frac{3}{10}$ ℓ = ⬜ ml

(f) $4\frac{1}{3}$ min = ⬜ s

(g) $2\frac{1}{10}$ km = ⬜ m

(h) $3\frac{1}{3}$ h = ⬜ min

(i) $5\frac{3}{4}$ ft = ⬜ in.

Exercise 11, pages 68 - 69

16. (a) What fraction of $2 is 80¢?

$2 = 200¢

$1 = 100¢

$\frac{80}{200}$ = ⬜

(b) Express 600 ml as a fraction of 1 liter.
(c) Express 90 cm as a fraction of 3 m.
(d) Express 45 seconds as a fraction of 1 minute.
(e) Express 50 minutes as a fraction of 2 hours.

Exercise 12, pages 70 - 71

PRACTICE D

Find the value of each of the following in its simplest form.

	(a)	(b)	(c)
1.	$\frac{1}{2} \times 14$	$\frac{1}{4} \times 26$	$\frac{2}{5} \times 40$
2.	$30 \times \frac{4}{5}$	$40 \times \frac{2}{3}$	$15 \times \frac{5}{9}$
3.	$\frac{7}{3} \times 21$	$\frac{13}{5} \times 20$	$40 \times \frac{9}{8}$

Find the missing number in each 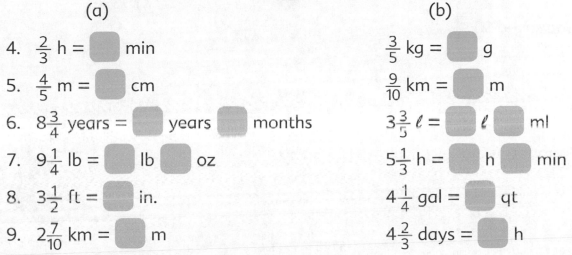.

(a)

4. $\frac{2}{3}$ h = ⬜ min

5. $\frac{4}{5}$ m = ⬜ cm

6. $8\frac{3}{4}$ years = ⬜ years ⬜ months

7. $9\frac{1}{4}$ lb = ⬜ lb ⬜ oz

8. $3\frac{1}{2}$ ft = ⬜ in.

9. $2\frac{7}{10}$ km = ⬜ m

(b)

$\frac{3}{5}$ kg = ⬜ g

$\frac{9}{10}$ km = ⬜ m

$3\frac{3}{5}$ ℓ = ⬜ ℓ ⬜ ml

$5\frac{1}{3}$ h = ⬜ h ⬜ min

$4\frac{1}{4}$ gal = ⬜ qt

$4\frac{2}{3}$ days = ⬜ h

10. (a) What fraction of $1 is 90¢?
    (b) What fraction of 2 ℓ is 750 ml?
    (c) What fraction of 3 lb is 12 oz?

11. (a) Express 9 months as a fraction of 1 year.
    (b) Express 50 minutes as a fraction of 2 hours.
    (c) Express 8 in. as a fraction of 2 ft.

12. In an examination, 40 out of 44 students passed. What fraction of the students passed the examination?

13. Holly earns $350 a month. She saves $70 each month. What fraction of her earnings does she save?

7 Word Problems

Melissa had $125. She spent $\frac{2}{5}$ of the money and saved the rest.

How much money did she save?

$$1 - \frac{2}{5} = \frac{3}{5}$$

She saved $\frac{3}{5}$ of the money.

First, I find what fraction of the money is saved.

$$\frac{3}{5} \times \$125 = \$\boxed{}$$

She saved $\boxed{}$.

Amount of money spent $= \dfrac{2}{\underset{1}{\cancel{5}}} \times \$\overset{25}{\cancel{125}} = \$50$

I do it in another way.

Amount of money saved $= \$125 - \$50 = \$\boxed{}$

$125

5 units $= \$125$

1 unit $= \$\boxed{}$

Here is yet another way. I find 1 unit first.

Amount of money saved $= 3$ units $= \$\boxed{}$

1. There are 96 children in a library. $\frac{5}{8}$ of them are girls. How many boys are there?

8 units = 96
3 units = ?

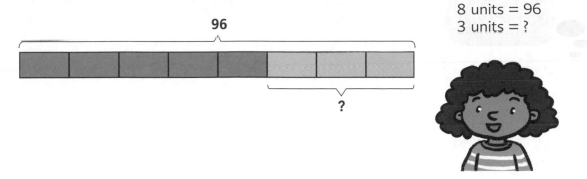

96

?

2. David had $40. He spent $\frac{1}{5}$ of the money on a storybook and $\frac{3}{10}$ on a calculator. How much did he spend altogether?

10 units = 40

5 units = ?

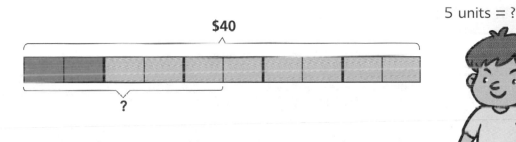

$40

?

3. Scott had some eggs. He sold $\frac{5}{8}$ of them. If he sold 300 eggs, how many eggs did he have at first?

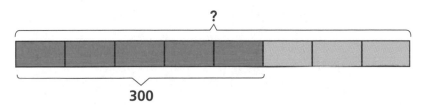

?

300

Exercise 13, pages 72 - 73
Exercise 14, pages 74 - 75

1. Brianna had 18 postcards. She gave $\frac{1}{3}$ of them to Mary. How many postcards did she have left?

2. 60 children went to the beach. $\frac{4}{5}$ of them could swim. How many children could not swim?

3. Mr. Garcia had 64 oranges. He kept $\frac{1}{4}$ of them and sold the rest. How many oranges did he sell?

4. John had $50. He spent $\frac{1}{5}$ of it on a book and $\frac{1}{10}$ on a flashlight. How much money did he have left?

5. Sally had $30. She spent $\frac{2}{3}$ of it on a watch and $4 on a book. How much money did she have left?

6. There were 320 students in an auditorium. $\frac{3}{5}$ of them were boys. How many more boys than girls were there?

7 $\frac{3}{7}$ of the apples in a box are red apples. The rest are green apples. There are 24 green apples. How many apples are there altogether?

8. After spending $\frac{2}{5}$ of his money on a video game, Josh had $42 left. How much money did he have at first?

REVIEW 3

1. Write the following in figures.
   (a) Five hundred fifteen thousand, four hundred seven
   (b) Four million, six hundred thousand

2. Write the following in words.
   (a) 872,520   (b) 1,034,000

3. What is the value of the digit 9 in 9,364,000?

4. (a) Round $437,549 to the nearest $1000.
   (b) Round 42,652 km to the nearest 1000 km.

5. A house is sold for about $2,400,000. Which one of the following could be the actual selling price of the house?
   $2,356,000 $2,299,000 $2,460,000 $2,310,000

6. (a) Write a common factor of 24 and 32.
   (b) Write a common multiple of 8 and 10.

7. Round each number to the nearest 1000.
   Then estimate the value of
   (a) 3472 + 1607   (b) 9035 − 5712

8. What is the missing number in each ▢ ?

   3,600,000, ▢ , 4,800,000, 5,400,000, ▢

9. Estimate the value of
   (a) 3268 × 7   (b) 4312 ÷ 6

10. Multiply or divide.
    (a) 2650 × 600   (b) 34,400 × 80   (c) 1290 ÷ 80
    (d) 52 × 75   (e) 994 ÷ 71   (f) 301 ÷ 24

11. Find the value of each of the following.
    (a) $2 \times (28 + 36) - 49$ (b) $78 + 21 \div 3 - (6 + 25)$
    (c) $50 - (225 \div 15 + 13)$ (d) $29 + (300 \div 10 - 3 \times 9)$

12. Fill in the missing number.

    $95 \times 8 = (100 \times 8) - (\boxed{} \times 8)$

13. Find the value of $5^2 \times 7^2$.

14. Find the prime factorization of 72.

15. Write each fraction in its simplest form.
    (a) $\frac{6}{8}$ (b) $\frac{9}{15}$

16. Express each of the following as an improper fraction.
    (a) $5\frac{3}{8}$ (b) $3\frac{7}{11}$

17. Express each of the following as a whole number or a mixed number in its simplest form.
    (a) $\frac{20}{6}$ (b) $\frac{16}{4}$

18. Name two equivalent fractions for each of these fractions.
    (a) $\frac{3}{4}$ (b) $\frac{2}{6}$

19. Divide. Express each answer as a fraction in its simplest form.
    (a) $8 \div 12$ (b) $15 \div 54$

20. Which is greater?
    (a) $\frac{3}{2}$ or $\frac{5}{4}$ (b) $2\frac{1}{2}$ or $2\frac{1}{7}$ (c) $3\frac{8}{9}$ or 4

21. Arrange the fractions in order, beginning with the smallest.
    $1\frac{3}{4}, \frac{9}{4}, 1\frac{5}{8}, \frac{9}{2}$

22. What number must be added to $4\frac{2}{9}$ to make 5?

23. Add or subtract. Give each answer in its simplest form.
    (a) $\frac{5}{6} + \frac{3}{4}$ (b) $2\frac{1}{2} + 5\frac{4}{5}$ (c) $4\frac{3}{4} - \frac{2}{3}$

24. Multiply or divide.

 (a) $\frac{7}{20} \times 4$

 (b) $24 \times \frac{5}{8}$

 (c) $35 \times \frac{2}{5}$

25. (a) Express $\frac{3}{5}$ m in centimeters.

 (b) Express $1\frac{7}{10}$ kg in kilograms and grams.

 (c) Express $2\frac{3}{4}$ lb in pounds and ounces.

26. Ashley had 600 stickers. She packed them into packets of 24. How many packets of stickers did she get?

27. There are 2204 children in a school. 925 of them are girls. How many more boys than girls are there?

28. 3 pieces of ribbon, each 85 cm long, are cut from a length of ribbon 3 m long. What is the length of the remaining piece of ribbon?

29. Peter, John and Dan shared $1458 equally. Peter used part of his share to buy a bicycle and had $139 left. What was the cost of the bicycle?

30. Bonita bought $2\frac{1}{5}$ kg of potatoes and $1\frac{1}{2}$ kg of carrots. How much more potatoes than carrots did she buy?

31. There are 42 students in Miss Brown's class. $\frac{3}{7}$ of them wear glasses. How many students wear glasses?

32. Danny bought 6 cartons of drink. Each carton contained $\frac{1}{4}$ liter of drink. Find the total amount of drink in liters.

Review 3, pages 76 - 78

4 MULTIPLY AND DIVIDE FRACTIONS

1 Product of Fractions

Color $\frac{3}{4}$ of a rectangle.

Cut out $\frac{1}{2}$ of the colored parts.
What fraction of the rectangle is cut out?

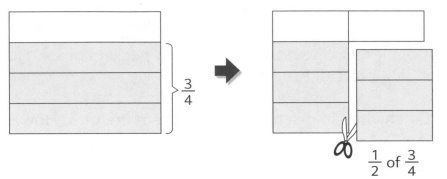

$\frac{1}{2}$ of $\frac{3}{4} = \frac{3}{8}$

$\frac{3}{8}$ of the rectangle is cut out.

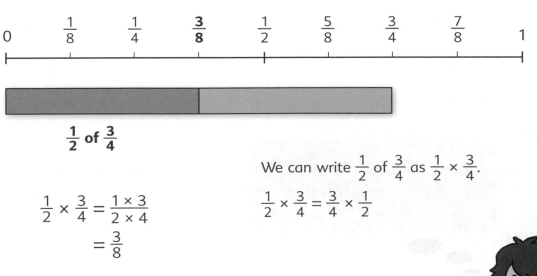

$\frac{1}{2}$ of $\frac{3}{4}$

$\frac{1}{2} \times \frac{3}{4} = \frac{1 \times 3}{2 \times 4}$

$\qquad = \frac{3}{8}$

We can write $\frac{1}{2}$ of $\frac{3}{4}$ as $\frac{1}{2} \times \frac{3}{4}$.

$\frac{1}{2} \times \frac{3}{4} = \frac{3}{4} \times \frac{1}{2}$

1. A flower garden occupies $\frac{1}{2}$ of a piece of land. $\frac{3}{5}$ of the garden is used for growing orchids. What fraction of the land is used for growing orchids?

$\frac{3}{5} \times \frac{1}{2} = \boxed{}$

$\boxed{}$ of the land is used for growing orchids.

2. Mrs. Green bought $\frac{3}{5}$ lb of sugar. She used $\frac{3}{4}$ of it for a Science experiment. How much sugar did she use?

$\frac{3}{4} \times \frac{3}{5} = \boxed{}$

She used $\boxed{}$ lb of sugar.

3. Find the area of a rectangle measuring $\frac{1}{3}$ m by $\frac{5}{6}$ m.

$\frac{1}{3} \times \frac{5}{6} = \boxed{}$

The area of the rectangle is $\boxed{}$ m².

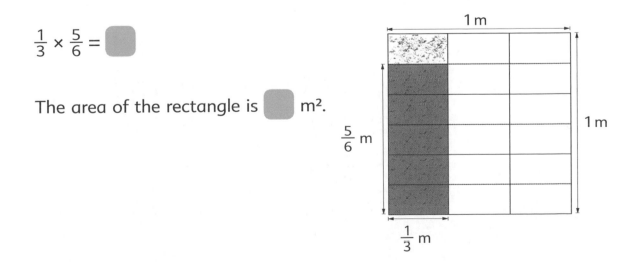

4. $\frac{2}{3}$ of a wall is painted red. $\frac{1}{4}$ of the remaining part is painted gray. What fraction of the wall is painted gray?

$1 - \frac{2}{3} = \frac{1}{3}$

The remaining part is $\frac{1}{3}$ of the wall.

$\frac{1}{4} \times \frac{1}{3} =$ ▢

▢ of the wall is painted gray.

Exercise 1, pages 79 - 80

5. Multiply $\frac{4}{5}$ by $\frac{2}{3}$.

$\frac{4}{5} \times \frac{2}{3} = \frac{4 \times 2}{5 \times 3}$

$=$ ▢

6. Find the product of $\frac{9}{10}$ and $\frac{5}{12}$.

Method 1:

$\frac{9}{10} \times \frac{5}{12} = \frac{{}^{3}\cancel{9} \times \cancel{5}^{1}}{{}_{2}\cancel{10} \times \cancel{12}_{4}}$

$=$ ▢

Method 2:

$\frac{{}^{3}\cancel{9}}{{}_{2}\cancel{10}} \times \frac{\cancel{5}^{1}}{\cancel{12}_{4}} = \frac{3 \times 1}{2 \times 4}$

$=$ ▢

7. Find the value of
   (a) $\frac{1}{2}$ of $\frac{1}{2}$
   (b) $\frac{1}{3}$ of $\frac{3}{4}$
   (c) $\frac{1}{4}$ of $\frac{8}{9}$

   (d) $\frac{5}{6} \times \frac{1}{5}$
   (e) $\frac{3}{4} \times \frac{5}{6}$
   (f) $\frac{4}{5} \times \frac{3}{8}$

   (g) $\frac{5}{8} \times \frac{4}{9}$
   (h) $\frac{1}{3} \times \frac{6}{7}$
   (i) $\frac{5}{6} \times \frac{7}{10}$

   (j) $\frac{15}{4} \times \frac{8}{3}$
   (k) $\frac{9}{4} \times \frac{16}{3}$
   (l) $\frac{12}{5} \times \frac{20}{9}$

Exercise 2, pages 81 - 82

Find the value of each of the following in its simplest form.

	(a)	(b)	(c)
1.	$\frac{3}{8} \times \frac{1}{3}$	$\frac{4}{9} \times \frac{5}{8}$	$\frac{7}{8} \times \frac{3}{7}$
2.	$\frac{2}{7} \times \frac{7}{10}$	$\frac{8}{9} \times \frac{3}{4}$	$\frac{9}{10} \times \frac{5}{6}$
3.	$\frac{5}{6} \times \frac{2}{5}$	$\frac{3}{4} \times \frac{2}{3}$	$\frac{3}{10} \times \frac{5}{6}$
4.	$\frac{16}{3} \times \frac{9}{4}$	$\frac{14}{9} \times \frac{12}{7}$	$\frac{10}{7} \times \frac{14}{5}$
5.	$\frac{20}{7} \times \frac{7}{4}$	$\frac{11}{5} \times \frac{20}{11}$	$\frac{15}{8} \times \frac{8}{3}$

6. Shawn had a piece of string $\frac{1}{2}$ m long. He used $\frac{1}{3}$ of it to tie a box. Find the length of the string which was used to tie the box.

7. Kelley had $\frac{3}{4}$ qt of cooking oil. She used $\frac{2}{5}$ of it to fry some fish. How much oil did she use?

8. Mrs. Ruiz bought $\frac{4}{5}$ kg of beef. She cooked $\frac{3}{4}$ of it for lunch. How much beef did she cook?

9. Sally ate $\frac{1}{6}$ of a fruit pie and gave $\frac{1}{5}$ of the remainder to her sister. What fraction of the fruit pie did she give away?

10. Find the area of a rectangle which measures $\frac{5}{8}$ m by $\frac{3}{5}$ m.

2 Word Problems

Jim had 360 stamps. He sold $\frac{1}{3}$ of them on Monday and $\frac{1}{4}$ of the remainder on Tuesday. How many stamps did he sell on Tuesday?

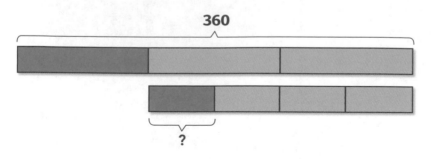

360

?

Method 1:

$$1 - \frac{1}{3} = \frac{2}{3}$$

First, I find what fraction of the stamps were left on Monday.

He had $\frac{2}{3}$ of the stamps left on Monday. The remainder is $\frac{2}{3}$.

$$\frac{1}{\cancel{4}_{2}} \times \frac{\cancel{2}^{1}}{3} = \frac{1}{2 \times 3}$$

$$= \frac{1}{6}$$

Next, I find $\frac{1}{4}$ of the remainder.

He sold $\frac{1}{6}$ of the stamps on Tuesday.

$$\frac{1}{6} \times 360 = \boxed{}$$

He sold  stamps on Tuesday.

Method 2:

$$1 - \frac{1}{3} = \frac{2}{3}$$

He had $\frac{2}{3}$ of the stamps left on Monday.

$$\frac{2}{\cancel{3}_1} \times \cancel{360}^{120} = 2 \times 120 = 240$$

I find the number of stamps left on Monday.

He had 240 stamps left on Monday.

$$\frac{1}{4} \times 240 = \boxed{}$$

He sold $\boxed{}$ stamps on Tuesday.

Method 3:

$$\frac{1}{\cancel{3}_1} \times \cancel{360}^{120} - 120$$

I find the number of stamps he sold on Monday first.

He sold 120 stamps on Monday.

$$360 - 120 = 240$$

He had 240 stamps left on Monday.

$$\frac{1}{4} \times 240 = \boxed{}$$

He sold $\boxed{}$ stamps on Tuesday.

I divide all the units into 2 parts, so there are now 6 parts.

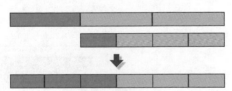

Method 4:

360

?

Total number of stamps = 6 units = 360

Number of stamps sold on Tuesday = 1 unit = $\boxed{}$

1. Marisol made 300 tarts. She sold $\frac{3}{4}$ of them and gave $\frac{1}{3}$ of the remainder to her neighbor. How many tarts did she have left?

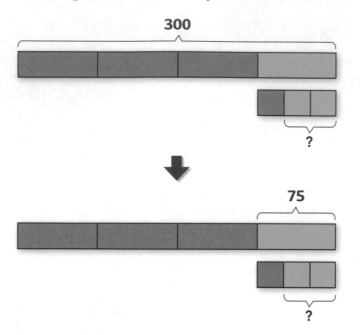

2. Mr. Anderson gave $\frac{2}{5}$ of his money to his wife and spent $\frac{1}{2}$ of the remainder. If he had $300 left, how much money did he have at first?

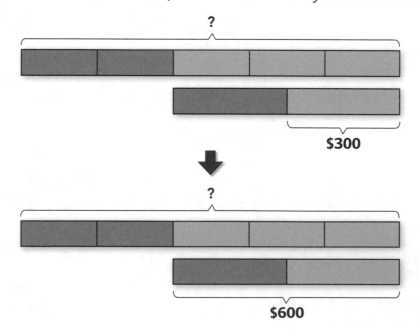

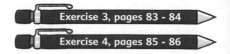

Exercise 3, pages 83 - 84
Exercise 4, pages 85 - 86

1. John had 300 stamps. He sold 120 stamps and gave $\frac{1}{3}$ of the rest to his brother.
   (a) How many stamps did he give to his brother?
   (b) How many stamps did he have left?

2. Mrs. Butler had 500 beads. She used $\frac{2}{5}$ of them to make some necklaces. Then she put the rest equally into 4 bottles. How many beads were there in each bottle?

3. Mr. Ray had $400. He spent $\frac{2}{5}$ of it on a vacuum cleaner and $\frac{1}{4}$ of the remainder on a fan. How much money did he have left?

4. A vendor sold $\frac{2}{3}$ of his sandwiches in the morning and $\frac{1}{6}$ in the afternoon. He sold 200 sandwiches altogether. How many sandwiches did he have left?

5. Mrs. Gray bought some eggs. She boiled $\frac{1}{2}$ of them and poached $\frac{1}{4}$ of the remainder. She had 9 eggs left. How many eggs did she buy?

6. Tyrone bought a bag of marbles. $\frac{1}{4}$ of the marbles were blue, $\frac{1}{8}$ were green and $\frac{1}{5}$ of the remainder were yellow. If there were 24 yellow marbles, how many marbles did he buy?

7. Rosa read 10 pages of a book on Monday. She read $\frac{1}{3}$ of the remainder on Tuesday. If she still had 24 pages to read, how many pages were there in the book?

3 Dividing a Fraction by a Whole Number

4 boys shared $\frac{2}{3}$ of a pizza equally.

What fraction of the pizza did each boy receive?

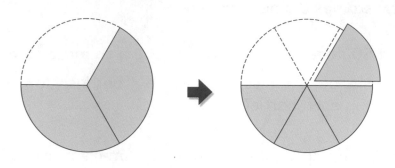

$$\frac{2}{3} \div 4 = \frac{1}{6}$$

Each boy received $\frac{1}{6}$ of the pizza.

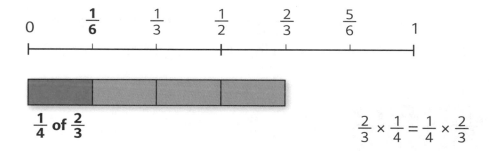

| 0 | $\frac{1}{6}$ | $\frac{1}{3}$ | $\frac{1}{2}$ | $\frac{2}{3}$ | $\frac{5}{6}$ | 1 |

$\frac{1}{4}$ **of** $\frac{2}{3}$

$\frac{2}{3} \times \frac{1}{4} = \frac{1}{4} \times \frac{2}{3}$

$\frac{2}{3} \div 4 = \frac{1}{4}$ of $\frac{2}{3}$ 　　or　　 $\frac{2}{3} \div 4 = \frac{{}^1 2}{3} \times \frac{1}{\cancel{4}_2}$

　　　　$= \frac{1}{\cancel{4}_2} \times \frac{\cancel{2}^1}{3}$ 　　　　　　　　$= \frac{1}{6}$

　　　　$= \frac{1}{6}$

1. Divide $\frac{2}{3}$ by 3.

   $\frac{2}{3} \div 3 = \frac{2}{3} \times \frac{1}{3}$

   $\qquad = \boxed{}$

   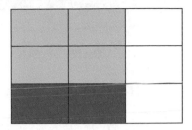

   Dividing by 3 is the same as multiplying by $\frac{1}{3}$.

2. Divide.

   (a) $\frac{3}{4} \div 6 = \frac{3}{4} \times \frac{1}{6}$

   $\qquad = \boxed{}$

   (b) $\frac{3}{5} \div 9 = \frac{3}{5} \times \frac{1}{9}$

   $\qquad = \boxed{}$

   (c) $\frac{5}{6} \div 5 = \frac{5}{6} \times \boxed{}$

   $\qquad = \boxed{}$

   (d) $\frac{9}{10} \div 3 = \frac{9}{10} \times \boxed{}$

   $\qquad = \boxed{}$

3. Find the value of each of the following in its simplest form.

   (a) $\frac{1}{3} \div 2$

   (b) $\frac{4}{5} \div 3$

   (c) $\frac{5}{7} \div 4$

   (d) $\frac{4}{5} \div 4$

   (e) $\frac{6}{7} \div 2$

   (f) $\frac{2}{3} \div 8$

   (g) $\frac{9}{16} \div 3$

   (h) $\frac{3}{8} \div 6$

   (i) $\frac{9}{10} \div 6$

   (j) $\frac{4}{9} \div 8$

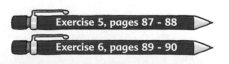

Exercise 5, pages 87 - 88

Exercise 6, pages 89 - 90

Find the value of each of the following in its simplest form.

	(a)	(b)	(c)
1.	$\frac{1}{3} \div 3$	$\frac{5}{6} \div 3$	$\frac{9}{10} \div 3$
2.	$\frac{3}{4} \div 5$	$\frac{1}{5} \div 4$	$\frac{8}{9} \div 6$
3.	$\frac{2}{5} \div 3$	$\frac{5}{9} \div 5$	$\frac{5}{6} \div 10$

4. A string of length $\frac{4}{5}$ m is cut into 2 equal pieces. What is the length of each piece?

5. $\frac{4}{5}$ of the money collected at a garage sale was divided equally among 4 clubs. What fraction of the money did each club receive?

6. 6 cartons of drinks weigh $\frac{3}{10}$ kg. Find the weight of 1 carton of drink.

7. Sara poured $\frac{2}{5}$ pt of fruit juice equally into 4 cups. How much fruit juice was there in each cup?

8. The perimeter of a square is $\frac{3}{4}$ m. Find the length of each side in meters.

9. Mrs. Jones divided $\frac{3}{4}$ kg of grapes equally among 6 children. How many kilograms of grapes did each child receive?

10. Jeff gave $\frac{1}{4}$ of a sum of money to his wife. Then he divided the remainder equally among his 4 children.
    (a) What fraction of the sum of money did each child receive?
    (b) If each child received $600, find the sum of money.

4 Dividing by a Fraction

Azizah bought 3 oranges. She cut each orange into halves. How many pieces of orange did she have?

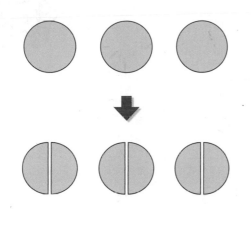

There are 2 halves in 1 whole.
There are 6 halves in 3 wholes.

$$3 \div \frac{1}{2} = 6$$

She had 6 pieces of orange.

$$3 \div \frac{1}{2} = 3 \times 2$$
$$= 6$$

2 is the reciprocal of $\frac{1}{2}$.

Dividing by $\frac{1}{2}$ is the same as multiplying by 2.

1. Divide 2 by $\frac{1}{3}$.

$2 \div \frac{1}{3} = 2 \times 3$

$\quad = $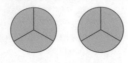

How many thirds are there in 2 wholes?

2. Divide.

(a) $1 \div \frac{1}{4} = 1 \times \boxed{}$

$\quad = \boxed{}$

(b) $2 \div \frac{1}{5} = 2 \times \boxed{}$

$\quad = \boxed{}$

3. Divide.

(a) $4 \div \frac{1}{2}$ (b) $6 \div \frac{1}{6}$ (c) $3 \div \frac{1}{7}$

(d) $8 \div \frac{1}{4}$ (e) $5 \div \frac{1}{3}$ (f) $9 \div \frac{1}{9}$

4. Divide 4 by $\frac{1}{2}$.

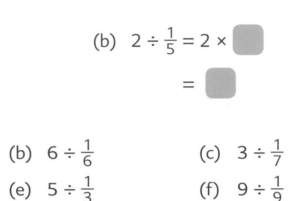

How many $\frac{1}{2}$'s can be made from 4 wholes?

$4 \div \frac{1}{2} = 4 \times 2$

$\quad = \boxed{}$

Dividing by $\frac{1}{2}$ is the same as multiplying by 2.

2 is the reciprocal of $\frac{1}{2}$.

Exercise 7, pages 91 - 92

5. Divide $\frac{1}{2}$ by $\frac{1}{4}$.

Divide $\frac{1}{2}$ into fourths.
There are 2 fourths.

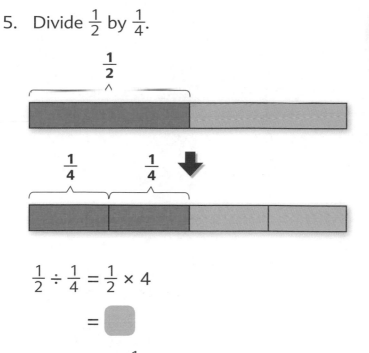

$\frac{1}{2} \div \frac{1}{4} = \frac{1}{2} \times 4$

$\phantom{\frac{1}{2} \div \frac{1}{4}} = \boxed{}$

Dividing by $\frac{1}{4}$ is the same as multiplying by 4.

4 is the reciprocal of $\frac{1}{4}$.

6. Divide.

(a) $\frac{2}{3} \div \frac{1}{3} = \frac{2}{3} \times \boxed{}$

$\phantom{\frac{2}{3} \div \frac{1}{3}} = \boxed{}$

(b) $\frac{2}{3} \div \frac{1}{6} = \frac{2}{3} \times \boxed{}$

$\phantom{\frac{2}{3} \div \frac{1}{6}} = \boxed{}$

7. Divide.

(a) $\frac{1}{4} \div \frac{1}{2}$

(b) $\frac{2}{5} \div \frac{1}{10}$

(c) $\frac{3}{4} \div \frac{1}{8}$

(d) $\frac{5}{6} \div \frac{1}{6}$

(e) $\frac{2}{9} \div \frac{1}{3}$

(f) $\frac{3}{8} \div \frac{1}{4}$

Exercise 8, page 93

8. Divide 3 by $\frac{3}{4}$.

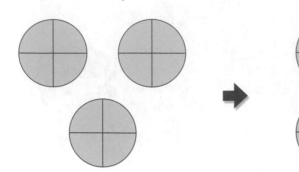 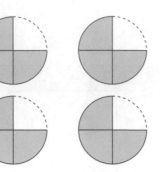

How many $\frac{3}{4}$'s can be made from 3 wholes?

$3 \div \frac{3}{4} = 3 \times \frac{4}{3}$

$\quad = \boxed{}$

Dividing by $\frac{3}{4}$ is the same as multiplying by $\frac{4}{3}$.

$\frac{4}{3}$ is the reciprocal of $\frac{3}{4}$.

9. Divide.
   (a) $1 \div \frac{3}{8} = 1 \times \boxed{}$

   $\quad\quad\quad = \boxed{}$

   (b) $2 \div \frac{4}{5} = 2 \times \boxed{}$

   $\quad\quad\quad = \boxed{}$

10. Divide.
    (a) $3 \div \frac{2}{3}$
    (b) $6 \div \frac{3}{5}$
    (c) $4 \div \frac{6}{7}$

Exercise 9, page 94

11. Divide 3 by $\frac{2}{3}$.

How many $\frac{2}{3}$'s can be made from 3 wholes?

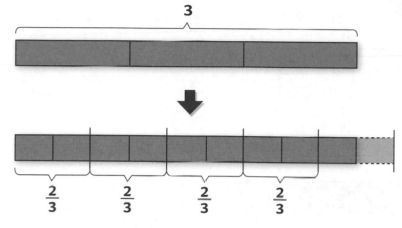

$\frac{2}{3}$ $\frac{2}{3}$ $\frac{2}{3}$ $\frac{2}{3}$

There are four $\frac{2}{3}$'s, and another half of a $\frac{2}{3}$ in 3.

So there are four-and-a-half $\frac{2}{3}$'s in 3.

$$3 \div \frac{2}{3} = 3 \times \frac{3}{2}$$

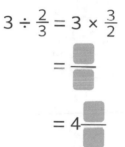

$$= \frac{\boxed{}}{\boxed{}}$$

$$= 4\frac{\boxed{}}{\boxed{}}$$

Dividing by $\frac{2}{3}$ is the same as multiplying by $\frac{3}{2}$.

$\frac{3}{2}$ is the reciprocal of $\frac{2}{3}$.

12. Divide $\frac{3}{4}$ by $\frac{3}{8}$.

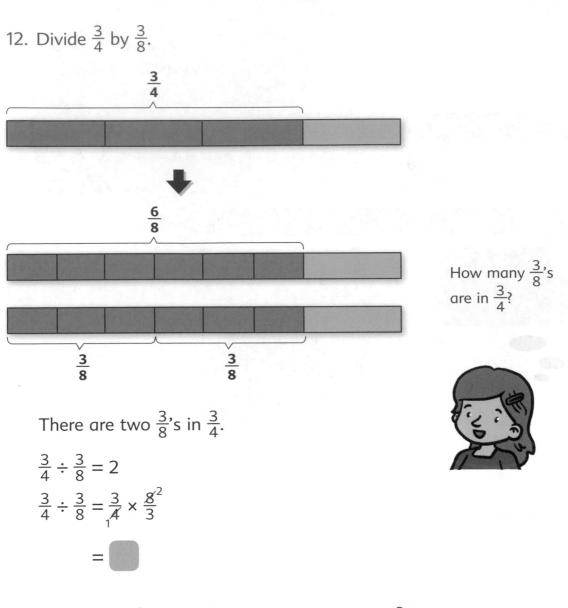

$\frac{3}{4}$

$\frac{6}{8}$

How many $\frac{3}{8}$'s
are in $\frac{3}{4}$?

$\frac{3}{8}$ $\frac{3}{8}$

There are two $\frac{3}{8}$'s in $\frac{3}{4}$.

$\frac{3}{4} \div \frac{3}{8} = 2$

$\frac{3}{4} \div \frac{3}{8} = \frac{3}{\underset{1}{4}} \times \frac{\overset{2}{8}}{3}$

$= \square$

Dividing by $\frac{3}{8}$ is the same as multiplying by $\frac{8}{3}$.

$\frac{8}{3}$ is the reciprocal of $\frac{3}{8}$.

96

13. Divide $\frac{3}{4}$ by $\frac{5}{8}$.

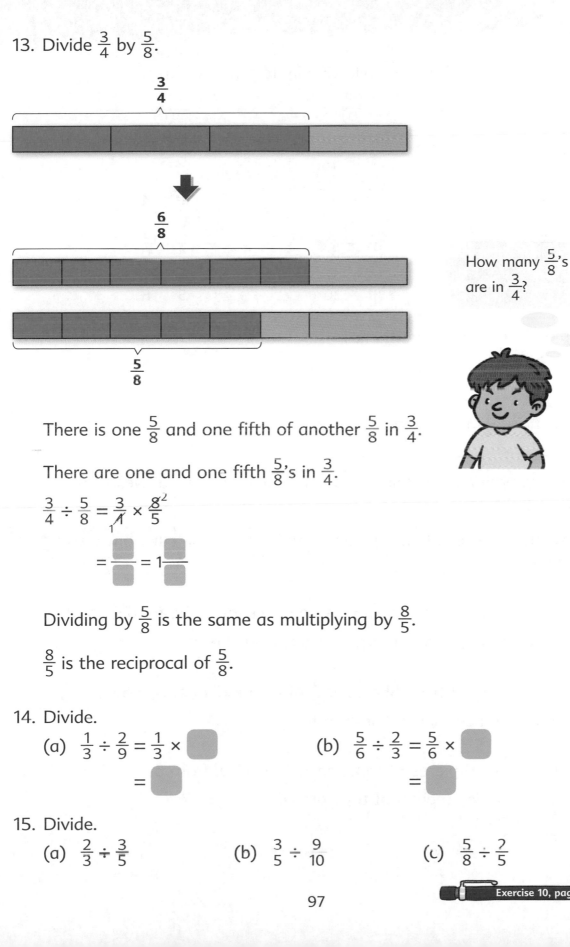

$$\frac{3}{4}$$

$$\frac{6}{8}$$

How many $\frac{5}{8}$'s are in $\frac{3}{4}$?

$$\frac{5}{8}$$

There is one $\frac{5}{8}$ and one fifth of another $\frac{5}{8}$ in $\frac{3}{4}$.

There are one and one fifth $\frac{5}{8}$'s in $\frac{3}{4}$.

$$\frac{3}{4} \div \frac{5}{8} = \frac{3}{\underset{1}{4}} \times \frac{\overset{2}{8}}{5}$$

$$= \frac{\square}{\square} = 1\frac{\square}{\square}$$

Dividing by $\frac{5}{8}$ is the same as multiplying by $\frac{8}{5}$.

$\frac{8}{5}$ is the reciprocal of $\frac{5}{8}$.

14. Divide.

   (a) $\frac{1}{3} \div \frac{2}{9} = \frac{1}{3} \times \boxed{}$

   $= \boxed{}$

   (b) $\frac{5}{6} \div \frac{2}{3} = \frac{5}{6} \times \boxed{}$

   $= \boxed{}$

15. Divide.

   (a) $\frac{2}{3} \div \frac{3}{5}$

   (b) $\frac{3}{5} \div \frac{9}{10}$

   (c) $\frac{5}{8} \div \frac{2}{5}$

97

Exercise 10, page 95

PRACTICE D

Find the value of each of the following in its simplest form.

	(a)	(b)	(c)
1.	$3 \div \frac{1}{2}$	$5 \div \frac{1}{4}$	$6 \div \frac{2}{3}$
2.	$\frac{1}{5} \div 2$	$\frac{1}{2} \div 6$	$\frac{2}{7} \div 4$
3.	$\frac{1}{4} \div \frac{1}{2}$	$\frac{8}{9} \div \frac{1}{3}$	$\frac{3}{4} \div \frac{1}{6}$
4.	$\frac{1}{6} \div \frac{2}{3}$	$\frac{3}{4} \div \frac{9}{10}$	$\frac{4}{5} \div \frac{5}{8}$

5. (a) How many $\frac{1}{6}$'s are there in 3?

   (b) How many $\frac{1}{6}$'s are there in $\frac{2}{3}$?

6. How many $\frac{1}{2}$-hour periods will make up 4 hours?

7. How many bricks weighing $\frac{1}{4}$ lb each will have a total weight of 3 lb?

8. How many pieces of string, each $\frac{1}{5}$ m long, can be cut from a string 3 m long?

9. Nicole used 6 m of string to tie some packages. She used $\frac{2}{3}$ m of string for each package. How many packages did she tie?

10. Holly had 2 kg of beef. She used $\frac{4}{5}$ of it to make stew. How many kilograms of beef did she have left?

11. Kimberly cuts 6 pieces of tape, each $\frac{4}{5}$ m long, from a roll of tape 5 m long. How many meters of tape are left in the roll?

⑤ More Word Problems

A tank is $\frac{1}{5}$ full. When another 700 ml of water is poured into the tank, it becomes $\frac{2}{3}$ full.

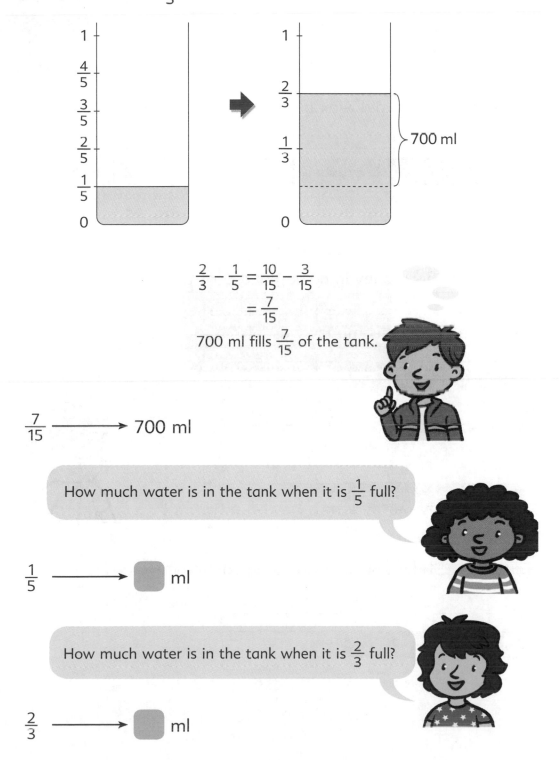

$$\frac{2}{3} - \frac{1}{5} = \frac{10}{15} - \frac{3}{15}$$
$$= \frac{7}{15}$$

700 ml fills $\frac{7}{15}$ of the tank.

$\frac{7}{15}$ ⟶ 700 ml

How much water is in the tank when it is $\frac{1}{5}$ full?

$\frac{1}{5}$ ⟶ ▢ ml

How much water is in the tank when it is $\frac{2}{3}$ full?

$\frac{2}{3}$ ⟶ ▢ ml

1. Alex bought some chairs. $\frac{1}{3}$ of them were red and $\frac{1}{4}$ were blue.
   The remaining 35 chairs were yellow.
   (a) What fraction of the chairs were yellow?

   $$1 - \frac{1}{3} - \frac{1}{4} = \frac{5}{12}$$

   (b) How many chairs did Alex buy?

   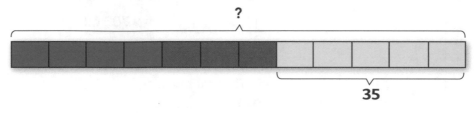

2. Max spent $\frac{3}{5}$ of his money in a shop and $\frac{1}{4}$ of the remainder in
   another shop.
   (a) What fraction of his money was left?

   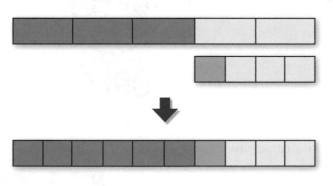

   $$\frac{3}{4} \text{ of } \frac{2}{5} = \frac{3}{4} \times \frac{2}{5}$$
   $$= \frac{3}{10}$$

   (b) If he had $90 left, how much money did he have at first?

   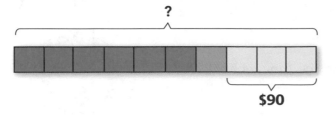

Exercise 11, pages 96 - 97

3. Megan spent $\frac{2}{5}$ of her money on a doll and $\frac{1}{2}$ of the remainder on a musical box. She spent $8 more on the doll than on the musical box. How much money did she have left?

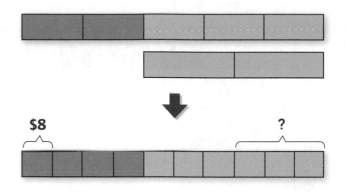

4. Lindsey read $\frac{2}{5}$ of a book on Monday. She read 12 pages on Tuesday. If she still had $\frac{1}{2}$ of the book to read, how many pages were there in the book?

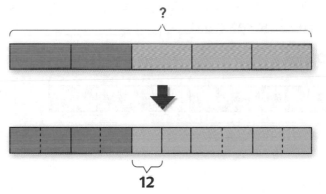

1 unit = 12

10 units =

5. $\frac{1}{4}$ of the beads in a box are red. There are 24 more yellow beads than red beads. The remaining 76 beads are blue. How many beads are there altogether?

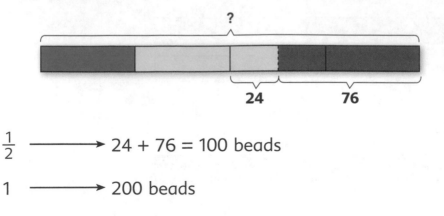

$\frac{1}{2} \longrightarrow$ 24 + 76 = 100 beads

1 $\longrightarrow$ 200 beads

There were 200 beads altogether.

6. 10 jugs of water can fill $\frac{5}{8}$ of a bucket. Another 4 jugs and 5 cups of water are needed to fill the remaining part of the bucket. How many cups of water can the bucket hold?

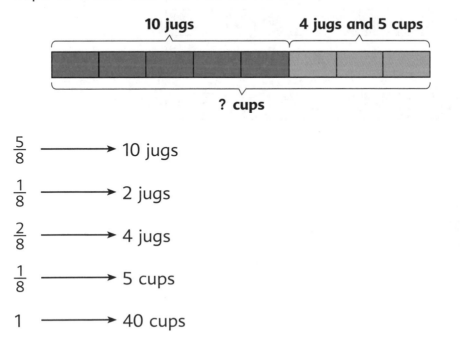

$\frac{5}{8} \longrightarrow$ 10 jugs

$\frac{1}{8} \longrightarrow$ 2 jugs

$\frac{2}{8} \longrightarrow$ 4 jugs

$\frac{1}{8} \longrightarrow$ 5 cups

1 $\longrightarrow$ 40 cups

The bucket can hold 40 cups of water.

Exercise 12, pages 98 - 101

1. There are 300 passengers on board an airplane. $\frac{2}{3}$ of them are men, $\frac{1}{4}$ are women and the rest are children. How many children are there?

2. There are 350 members in a swimming club. $\frac{2}{7}$ of them are new members. $\frac{3}{10}$ of the new members are females. How many new female members are there?

3. Sally made 500 gingerbread men. She sold $\frac{3}{4}$ of them and gave away $\frac{2}{5}$ of the remainder. How many gingerbread men did she give away?

4. Dani made some sandwiches for a party. $\frac{3}{5}$ of them were chicken sandwiches and the rest were tuna sandwiches. There were 240 tuna sandwiches. How many chicken sandwiches were there?

5. After paying $30 for a shirt, David had $\frac{3}{5}$ of his money left. How much money did he have at first?

6. After spending $\frac{2}{5}$ of his money on a storybook, Matthew had $12 left. How much did he spend on the storybook?

7. Greg spent $\frac{1}{4}$ of his money on a typewriter. If the typewriter cost $120, how much money did he have at first?

8. Cameron has 480 stamps. $\frac{5}{8}$ of them are U.S. stamps and the rest are foreign stamps. How many more U.S. stamps than foreign stamps does he have?

9. Taylor bought 24 lb of flour. She used $\frac{1}{3}$ of it to bake fruit pies and $\frac{1}{4}$ of the remainder to bake some bread. How many pounds of flour were left?

1. Write the following in words.
   (a) 4,500,000
   (b) 162,003

2. Which one of the following numbers has the digit 6 in the ten thousands place?
   6,541,000, 640,059, 546,109, 5,164,000

3. The population of Marina Town is 280,524. Round the number to the nearest 1000.

4. Round each number to the nearest 1000.
   Then estimate the value of
   (a) 29,074 + 5872
   (b) 14,236 − 6223

5. Estimate the value of
   (a) 4825 × 63
   (b) 7134 ÷ 82

6. Multiply or divide.
   (a) 1245 × 4000
   (b) 1280 ÷ 80
   (c) 84,000 ÷ 7000

7. Multiply or divide.
   (a) 36 × 28
   (b) 615 × 32
   (c) 864 ÷ 36

8. Find the value of each of the following.
   (a) 28 + 19 − 24
   (b) 12 − 9 × 5 ÷ 15
   (c) (42 + 14) ÷ 7 × 5
   (d) (59 + 13) ÷ (4 × 2)

9. Fill in the missing number ▊.

   (a) (29 × 4) = (25 × 4) + (▊ × 4)

   (b) (29 × 4) = (30 × 4) − (▊ × 4)

10. Write **>**, **<** or **=** in each ⬤.

  (a) 5^2 ⬤ 5×2

  (b) $3 \times 3 \times 2 \times 3 \times 7$ ⬤ $2 \times 3^4 \times 7$

  (c) 4×97 ⬤ $(100 \times 4) - (3 \times 4)$

  (d) $3^3 \times 7$ ⬤ $3 \times 3 \times 7$

11. Find the prime factorization of 68.

12. Write each fraction in its simplest form.

  (a) $\frac{16}{24}$ (b) $\frac{32}{40}$

13. Express each of the following as an improper fraction.

  (a) $4\frac{5}{9}$ (b) $2\frac{3}{4}$

14. Express each of the following as a whole number or a mixed number in its simplest form.

  (a) $\frac{33}{3}$ (b) $\frac{30}{8}$

15. Name two equivalent fractions for each of these fractions.

  (a) $\frac{5}{9}$ (b) $\frac{11}{14}$

16. Divide. Express each answer as a fraction in its simplest form.

  (a) $63 \div 18$ (b) $100 \div 35$

17. Which is greater?

  (a) $1\frac{6}{7}$ or $\frac{12}{7}$ (b) $4\frac{2}{3}$ or $\frac{9}{2}$ (c) $3\frac{1}{6}$ or $\frac{16}{5}$

18. Arrange the fractions in order, beginning with the smallest.

  $1\frac{2}{8}, \ \frac{36}{5}, \ 1\frac{2}{3}, \ \frac{8}{2}$

19. How many fourths are there in $3\frac{1}{4}$?

20. Add or subtract. Give each answer in its simplest form.

    (a) $3\frac{3}{8} + \frac{5}{12}$ (b) $6 - \frac{6}{7}$ (c) $6\frac{1}{3} - 2\frac{3}{5}$

21. Multiply or divide.

    (a) $\frac{3}{4} \times \frac{8}{9}$ (b) $\frac{5}{8} \times \frac{14}{15}$ (c) $\frac{8}{12} \times \frac{16}{20}$

    (d) $\frac{3}{5} \div 3$ (e) $\frac{7}{8} \div 2$ (f) $\frac{4}{7} \div 12$

22. (a) Express 4 months as a fraction of 1 year.

    (b) Express 48 minutes as a fraction of $1\frac{1}{2}$ hours.

    (c) Express 1 pt as a fraction of $3\frac{1}{2}$ qt.

23. Divide.

    (a) $8 \div \frac{1}{3}$ (b) $\frac{4}{6} \div 10$

    (c) $\frac{5}{9} \div \frac{1}{3}$ (d) $\frac{2}{7} \div \frac{4}{5}$

    (e) $8 \div \frac{2}{3}$ (f) $\frac{3}{8} \div \frac{3}{7}$

24. Oranges are packed in a box in 4 layers. Each layer has 6 rows of oranges with 8 oranges in each row. How many oranges are there in the box?

25. Mrs. McCall has 1400 tarts. If she sells all of them at 80 cents each, how much money will she receive?

26. Haley answered 28 out of 32 problems correctly. What fraction of the problems did she answer correctly?

27. Mrs. Meier had $\frac{3}{5}$ kg of sugar. She used $\frac{1}{4}$ of it to make fruit pies. How much sugar did she use to make the fruit pies?

28. Mrs. Law bought $\frac{1}{2}$ of a cake. She cut it into 4 equal pieces. What fraction of the whole cake is each piece?

29. Mr. Ricci spent $\frac{1}{3}$ of his salary on food and $\frac{2}{5}$ of the remainder on transport.
    (a) What fraction of his salary did he have left?
    (b) If he had $600 left, find his salary.

30. Nicole bought 6 m of cloth to make a skirt and 3 shirts. She used $1\frac{3}{4}$ m for the skirt and $\frac{3}{4}$ m for each shirt. How much cloth did she have left?

31. David had 1280 eggs. He sold $\frac{3}{5}$ of them on Saturday and $\frac{1}{4}$ of the remainder on Sunday. Find the total number of eggs sold on the two days.

32. Ryan withdrew $\frac{1}{4}$ of his savings from the bank. He spent $450 of it and had $150 left. How much money was his total savings in the bank at first?

33. Marlsa spent $\frac{3}{4}$ of her money on a necklace. She spent $\frac{1}{2}$ of the remainder on some earrings. The necklace cost $30 more than the earrings. How much did the necklace cost?

Review 4, pages 102 - 105

5 PERIMETER, AREA AND SURFACE AREA

1 Square Units

Find the area of each of these figures.

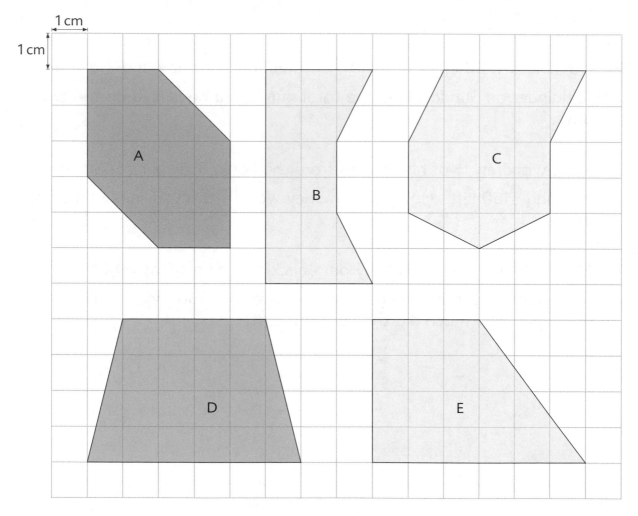

Which figure has the greatest area?
Which figure has the smallest area?
Which figures have the same area?

1.

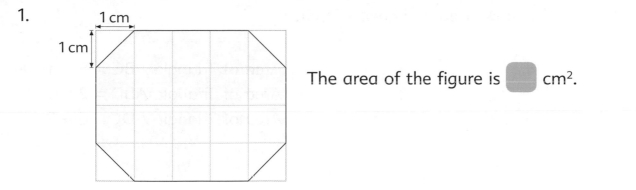

The area of the figure is ▢ cm².

2. Find the area of each shaded figure.

(a)

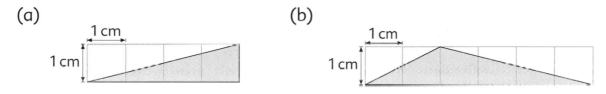

(b)

(c)

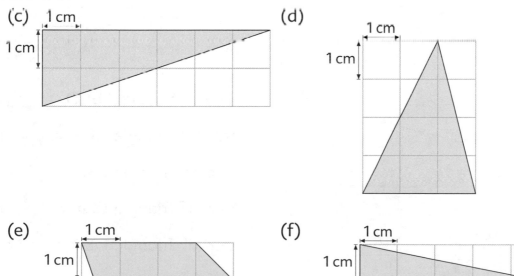

(d)

(e)

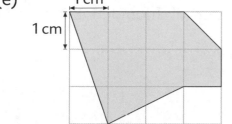

(f)

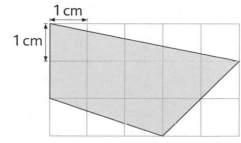

3. Find the area of each shaded triangle.

(a)

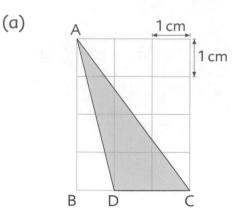

Area of Triangle ABC = 6 cm²
Area of Triangle ABD = 2 cm²
Area of Triangle ADC = 6 − 2

$$= \boxed{} \ cm^2$$

(b)

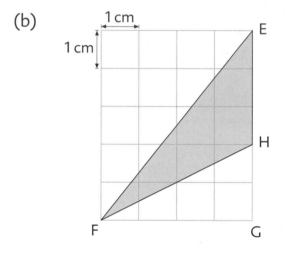

Area of Triangle EFG = $\boxed{}$ cm²

Area of Triangle FGH = $\boxed{}$ cm²

Area of Triangle EFH = $\boxed{}$ cm²

(c)

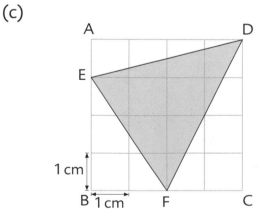

Area of Square ABCD = $\boxed{}$ cm²

Area of Triangle ADE = $\boxed{}$ cm²

Area of Triangle EBF = $\boxed{}$ cm²

Area of Triangle CDF = $\boxed{}$ cm²

Area of Triangle DEF = $\boxed{}$ cm²

Exercise 1, pages 106 - 107

② Rectangles and Squares

Find the area of the shaded figure.

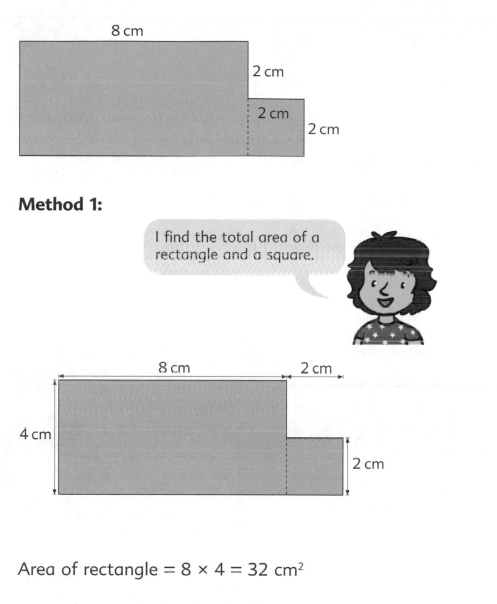

Method 1:

I find the total area of a rectangle and a square.

Area of rectangle = 8 × 4 = 32 cm²

Area of square = 2 × 2 = 4 cm²

Total area = 32 + 4 = ⬚ cm²

Method 2:

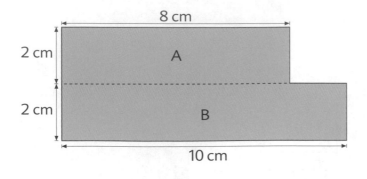

I find the total area of two rectangles.

Area of Rectangle A = 8 × 2 = 16 cm²

Area of Rectangle B = 10 × 2 = 20 cm²

Total area = 16 + 20 = ⬜ cm²

Method 3:

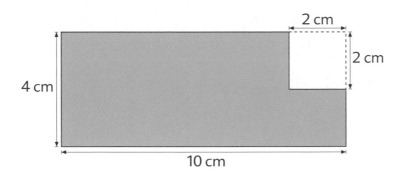

I subtract the area of a square from the area of a rectangle.

Area of rectangle = 10 × 4 = 40 cm²

Area of square = 2 × 2 = 4 cm²

Area of the shaded figure = 40 − 4 = ⬜ cm²

1. In each of the following figures, draw a straight line to divide the figure into two parts of equal area.

(a)

(b)

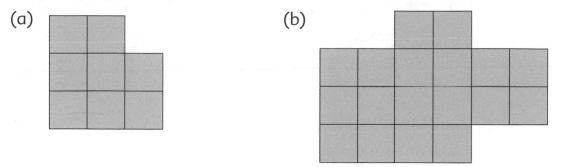

2. Find the area and perimeter of each figure.
   (All the lines meet at right angles.)

(a)

(b)

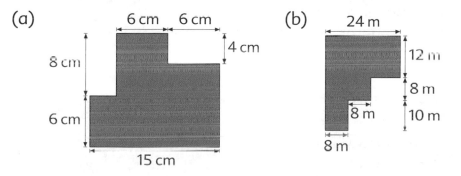

3. Find the shaded area of each rectangle.

(a)

(b)

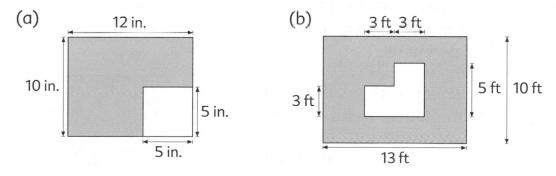

Exercise 2, page 108

1. Find the area of the shaded figure.

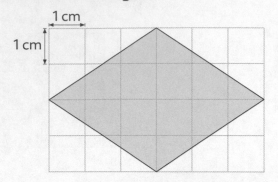

2. Gomez bought a piece of wire 2 m long.
   He used the wire to form squares of side 12 cm.

   (a) How many squares could he make?
   (b) How many centimeters of wire had he left?

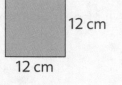

3. The figure shows a field with 5 sides.
   The lengths of 4 sides are given. If the
   perimeter of the field is 600 m, find
   the length of the 5th side.

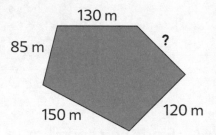

4. The area of a square is 36 cm².

   (a) Find the length of one side of the square.
   (b) Find its perimeter.

5. The area of a rectangle is 84 m². If its
   length is 12 m, find its width and perimeter.

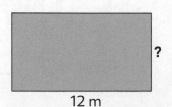

6. Find the shaded area of the rectangle.

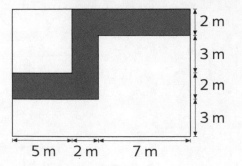

③ Area of a Triangle

Find the area of each shaded triangle and its related rectangle.

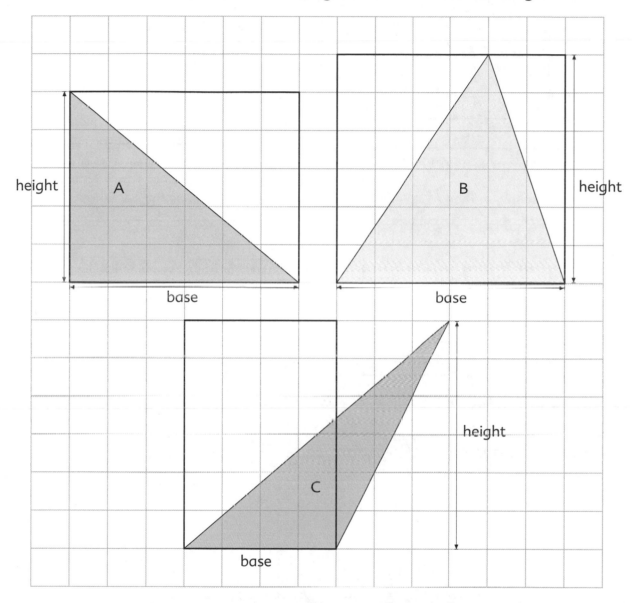

Compare the area of each triangle with the area of its related rectangle.

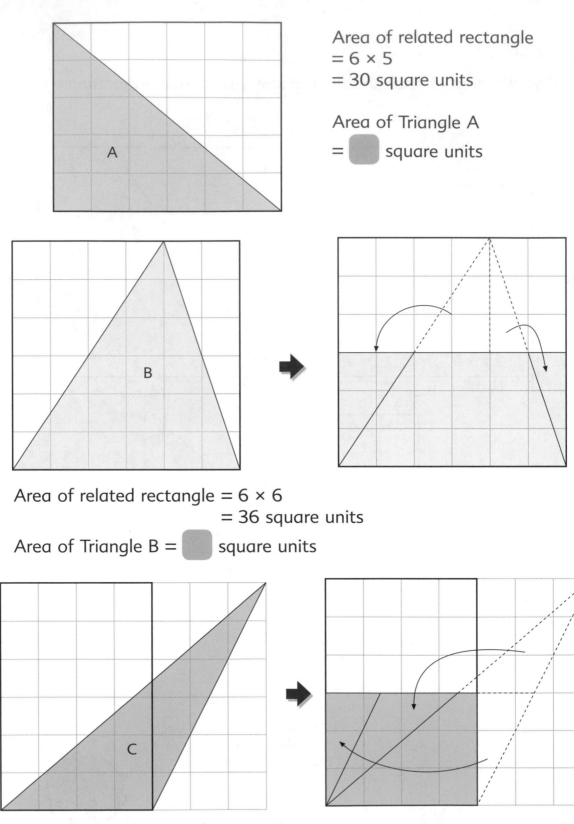

Area of related rectangle
= 6 × 5
= 30 square units

Area of Triangle A

= ▢ square units

Area of related rectangle = 6 × 6
= 36 square units

Area of Triangle B = ▢ square units

Area of related rectangle = 4 × 6
= 24 square units

Area of Triangle C = ▢ square units

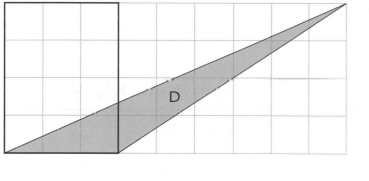

Area of related rectangle
= 3 × 4
= 12 square units

Area of Triangle D

$= \frac{1}{2} \times (9 \times 4) - \frac{1}{2} \times (6 \times 4)$

$= \frac{1}{2} \times (9 \times 4) - (6 \times 4)$

$= \frac{1}{2} \times (9 - 6) \times 4$

$= \frac{1}{2} \times 3 \times 4$

$=$ ⬛ square units

Area of triangle $= \frac{1}{2} \times$ Area of related rectangle

Area of triangle $= \frac{1}{2} \times$ base × height

$A = \frac{1}{2} \times b \times h$

1. For each of the following shaded triangles, name the height which is related to the given base of the triangle.

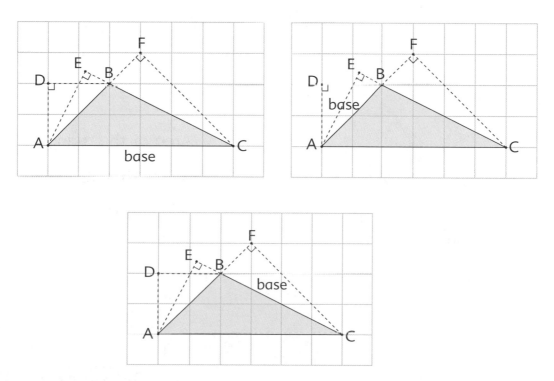

2. Find the area of each triangle.

(a)

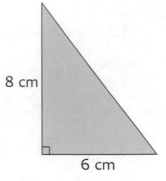

8 cm

6 cm

Area of the triangle

$= \frac{1}{2} \times 6 \times 8$

$= $ 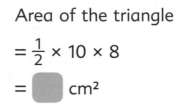 cm²

(b)

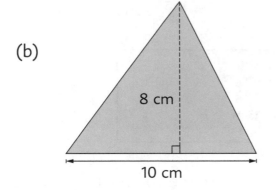

8 cm

10 cm

Area of the triangle

$= \frac{1}{2} \times 10 \times 8$

$= $ cm²

(c)

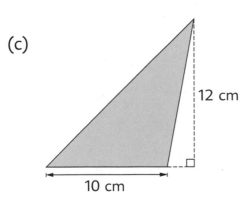

12 cm

10 cm

Area of the triangle

$= \frac{1}{2} \times 10 \times 12$

$= $ 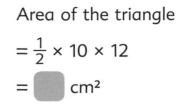 cm²

 Exercise 3, pages 109 - 112

3.

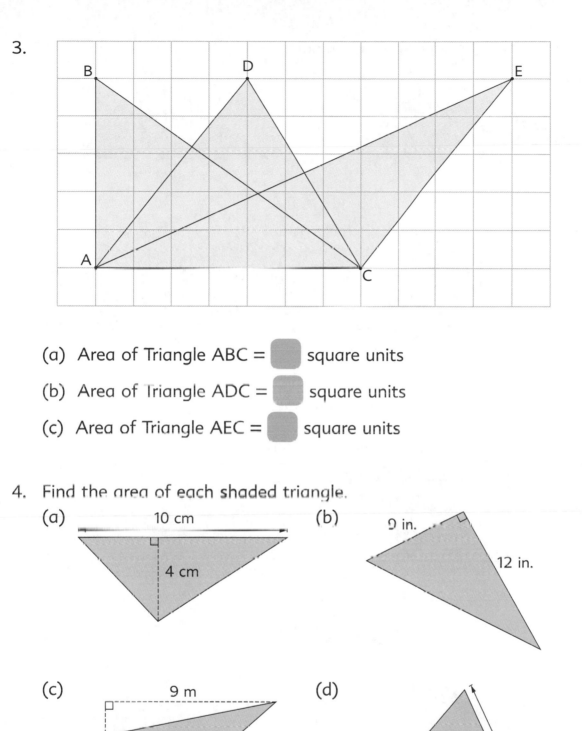

(a) Area of Triangle ABC = [ ] square units

(b) Area of Triangle ADC = [ ] square units

(c) Area of Triangle AEC = [ ] square units

4. Find the area of each shaded triangle.

(a) 10 cm

4 cm

(b) 9 in.

12 in.

(c) 9 m

7 m

(d) 20 ft

22 ft

Exercise 4, pages 113 - 115

5. Find the area of each shaded triangle.

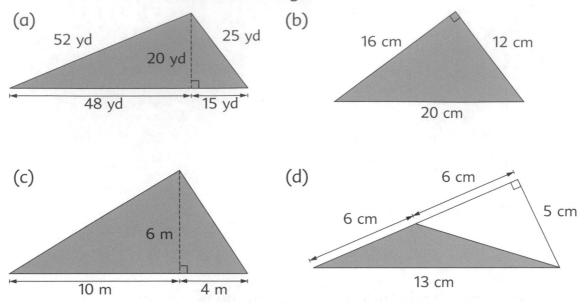

(a)

52 yd   20 yd   25 yd

48 yd   15 yd

(b)

16 cm   12 cm

20 cm

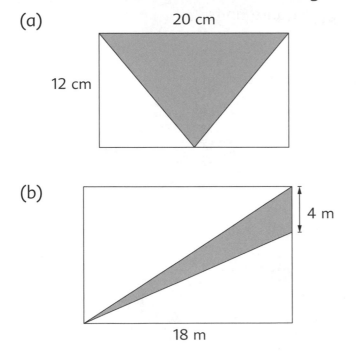

(c)

6 m

10 m   4 m

(d)

6 cm

6 cm   5 cm

13 cm

6. Find the shaded area of each rectangle.

(a)

20 cm

12 cm

(b)

4 m

18 m

7. Find the shaded area of each rectangle.

(a)

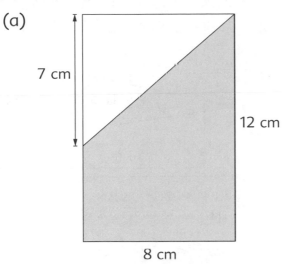

7 cm

12 cm

8 cm

In each figure, the unshaded part is a triangle.

Find the area of the triangle first.

(b)

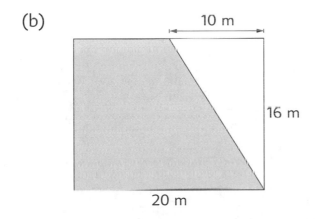

10 m

16 m

20 m

(c)

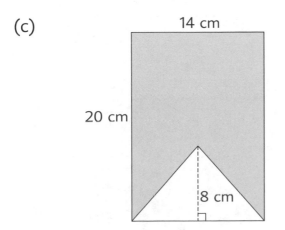

14 cm

20 cm

8 cm

Exercise 5, pages 116 - 118

1. Find the area of each shaded triangle.

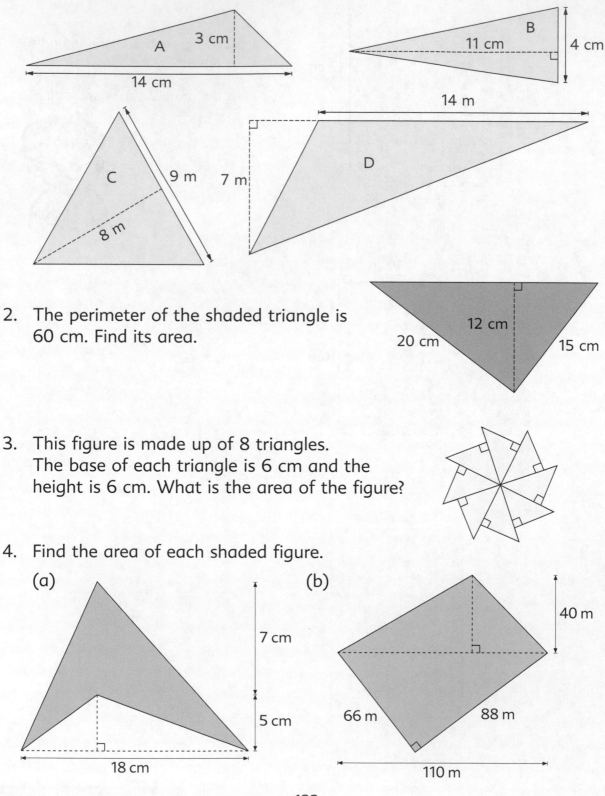

2. The perimeter of the shaded triangle is 60 cm. Find its area.

3. This figure is made up of 8 triangles. The base of each triangle is 6 cm and the height is 6 cm. What is the area of the figure?

4. Find the area of each shaded figure.

   (a)

   (b)

4 Area of a Parallelogram

Find the area of the parallelogram.

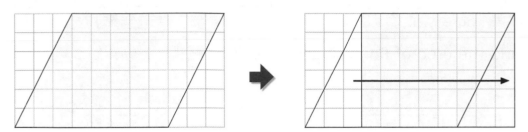

Compare the area of the parallelogram with the area of its related rectangle.

Area of rectangle = 8 × 6

$$= \boxed{} \text{ square units}$$

Area of parallelogram = $\boxed{}$ square units

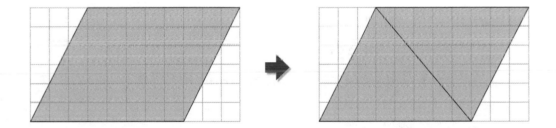

Divide the parallelogram into two congruent triangles.
Compare the area of the parallelogram with the area of the two triangles.

Area of one triangle $= \frac{1}{2} \times 8 \times 6$

$$= \boxed{} \text{ square units.}$$

Area of both triangles $= 2 \times \frac{1}{2} \times 8 \times 6$

$$= 8 \times 6$$

$$= \boxed{} \text{ square units}$$

Area of parallelogram = $\boxed{}$ square units

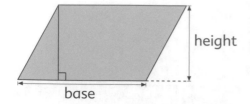

height

base

Area of parallelogram = base x height
$$A = b \times h$$

1. Find the area of Parallelogram ABCD.

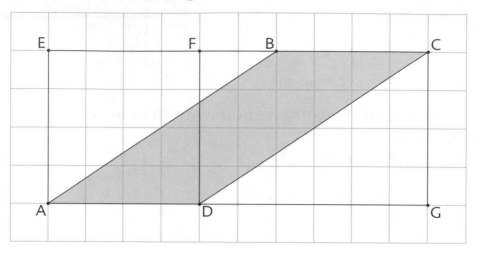

Method 1:

Area of Parallelogram ABCD

= Area of Rectangle AECG − area of Triangle AEB
   − area of Triangle DCG

$= 10 \times 4 - \frac{1}{2} \times (6 \times 4) - \frac{1}{2} \times (6 \times 4)$

$= 10 \times 4 - 6 \times 4$

$= (10 - 6) \times 4$

$= 4 \times 4$

= ⬚ square units

Method 2:

Area of Parallelogram ABCD

= base × height

= 4 × ⬚

= ⬚ square units

2. Find the area of each parallelogram.

(a)

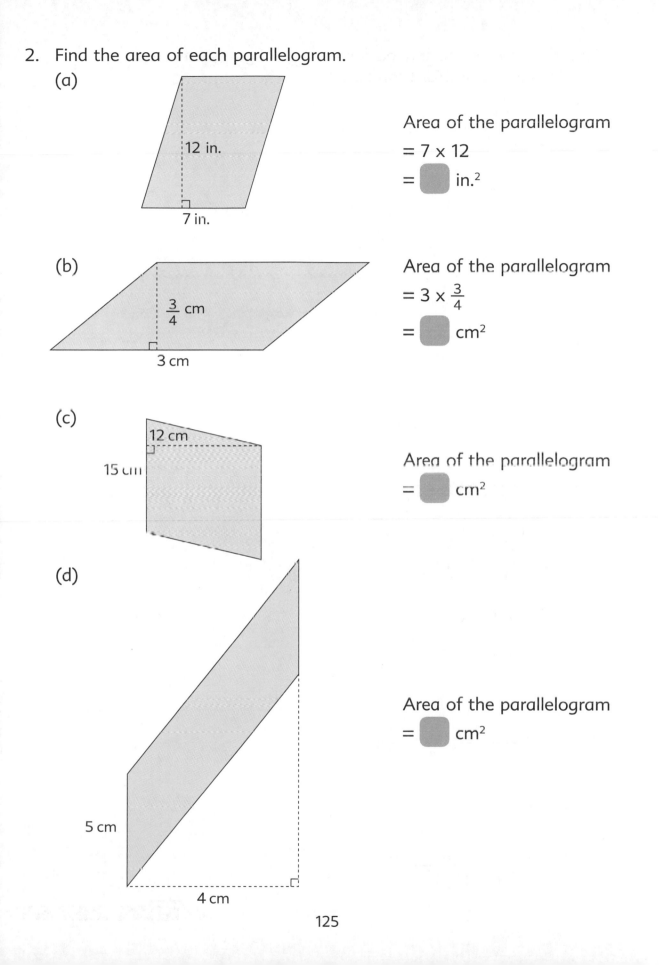

12 in.

7 in.

Area of the parallelogram

= 7 x 12

= ⬜ in.²

(b)

$\frac{3}{4}$ cm

3 cm

Area of the parallelogram

= 3 x $\frac{3}{4}$

= ⬜ cm²

(c)

12 cm

15 cm

Area of the parallelogram

= ⬜ cm²

(d)

5 cm

4 cm

Area of the parallelogram

= ⬜ cm²

3. Find the area of the shaded figures. Each figure is made from parallelograms and/or triangles.

(a)

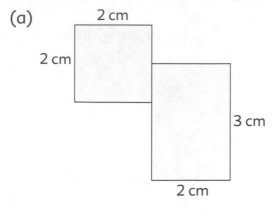

(b)

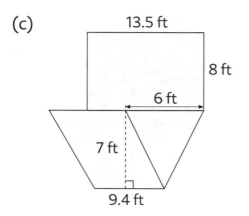

(c)

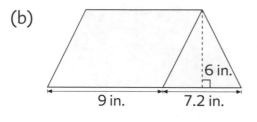

(d)

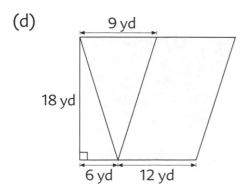

Exercise 6, pages 119 - 120

⑤ Surface Area

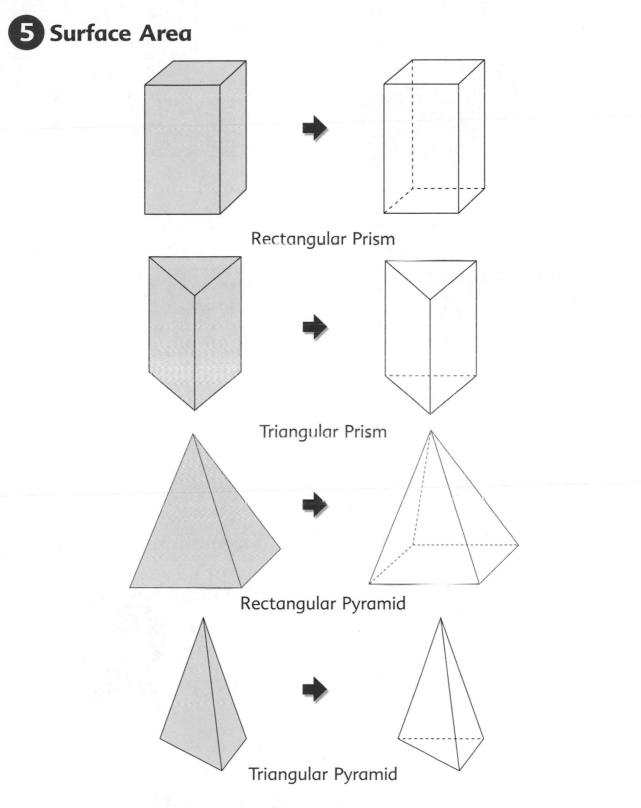

Rectangular Prism

Triangular Prism

Rectangular Pyramid

Triangular Pyramid

How many faces do each of these solids have?
What is the shape of each face?

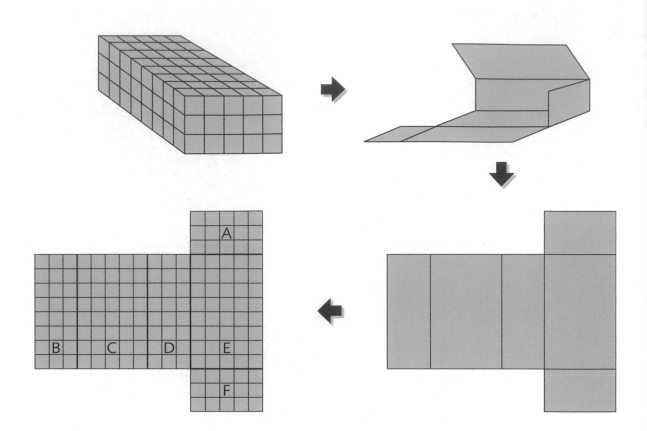

What is the area of each face?
What is the total area of all the faces?

The surface area of the rectangular prism is the sum of the area of all its faces.

1. Find the surface area of the rectangular prism.

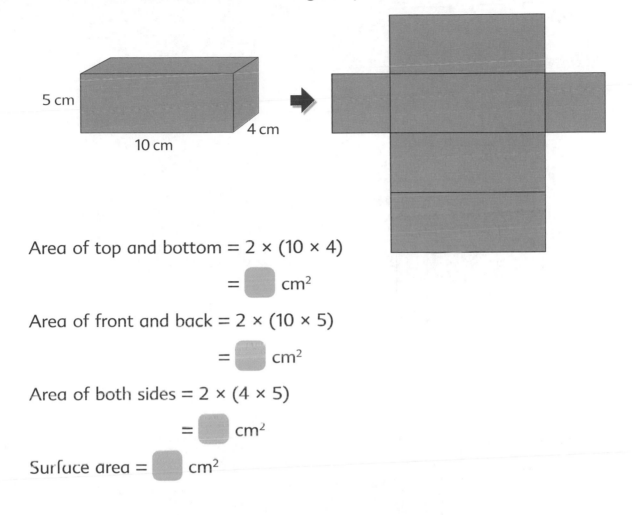

Area of top and bottom = 2 × (10 × 4)

= ☐ cm²

Area of front and back = 2 × (10 × 5)

= ☐ cm²

Area of both sides = 2 × (4 × 5)

= ☐ cm²

Surface area = ☐ cm²

2. Find the surface area of the cube.

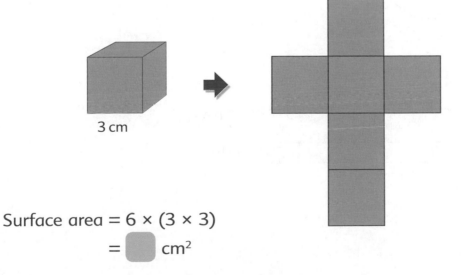

Surface area = 6 × (3 × 3)

= ☐ cm²

3. Find the surface area of each solid.

(a)

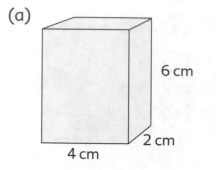

6 cm

2 cm

4 cm

(b)

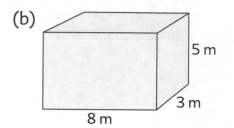

5 m

3 m

8 m

(c)

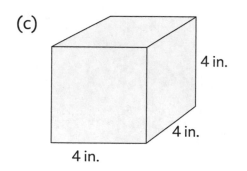

4 in.

4 in.

4 in.

(d)

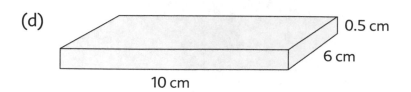

0.5 cm

6 cm

10 cm

 Exercise 7, pages 121 - 122

1. What number is 1000 less than 20,000?

2. Juan bought a car for $42,680. Round this amount of money to the nearest $1000.

3. Find the value of each of the following.
   (a) 670 × 10
   (b) 728 × 100
   (c) 350 × 1000
   (d) 4300 ÷ 10
   (e) 58,000 ÷ 100
   (f) 628,000 ÷ 1000

4. Find the value of each of the following.
   (a) 12 − 4 ÷ 2 + 6
   (b) 24 + 6 × 7 ÷ 3
   (c) (4 + 8) × 3 ÷ 4
   (d) 25 − (7 + 9 × 2) ÷ 5

5. Find the prime factorization of 120.

6. Divide.
   (a) $\frac{3}{5} \div \frac{6}{7}$
   (b) $\frac{2}{3} \div \frac{3}{5}$

7. If ☆☆☆☆☆ represent 60, what number do ☆☆ represent?

8. What fraction of 3 ℓ is 800 ml?

9. Steven had 24 pineapples. He sold 6 of them. What fraction of the pineapples did he sell?

10. An examination lasted $2\frac{1}{4}$ hours. Express $2\frac{1}{4}$ hours in hours and minutes.

11. A necklace is $\frac{3}{5}$ m long. Express $\frac{3}{5}$ m in centimeters.

12. Lily has $25. Mary has $10 more than Lily. Amber has 3 times as much money as Mary.
    (a) How much money does Amber have?
    (b) How much more money than Lily does Amber have?
    (c) How much money do the 3 girls have altogether?

13. Lynn bought 8 m of string. She used $\frac{5}{8}$ of the string to make a flower pot hanger. How much of the string did she have left?

14. Natalie cuts a raffia $\frac{4}{5}$ m long into 8 pieces of equal length. What is the length of each piece of raffia? Give the answer in meters.

15. Matthew had 64 watermelons. He sold $\frac{3}{4}$ of them. How many watermelons did he sell?

16. Mrs. Gray had 2 kg of flour. She used $\frac{2}{5}$ of it to make buns. How much flour did she have left? Give the answer in kilograms.

17. There are 1500 workers in a factory. $\frac{5}{6}$ of them are men. $\frac{3}{10}$ of the men are single. How much single male workers are there in the factory?

18. Lauren spent $\frac{3}{5}$ of her money on a refrigerator. The refrigerator cost $756. How much money did she have left?

19. Mrs. Stewart made some pies. She sold $\frac{3}{5}$ of them and gave $\frac{1}{4}$ of the remainder to the food bank. If she had 150 pies left, how many pies did she sell?

20. Susan spent $\frac{1}{4}$ of her money on a book and $\frac{1}{2}$ of the remainder on some paper. She spent $10 altogether. How much money did she have left?

21. Dan saved twice as much as Brett. Maria saved $60 more than Brett. If they saved $600 altogether, how much did Maria save?

22. Brett picked 257 cherries from one tree and 493 from another. He sold all the cherries at 50 for $3. How much money did he receive?

23. Charles bought 40 boxes of oranges for $258. There were 24 oranges in each box. He threw away 15 rotten oranges and sold the rest at 3 for $1. How much money did he make?

24. Find the area and the perimeter of the shaded figure.

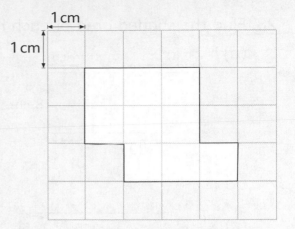

25. Find the perimeter and area of each figure. (All the lines meet at right angles.)

(a)

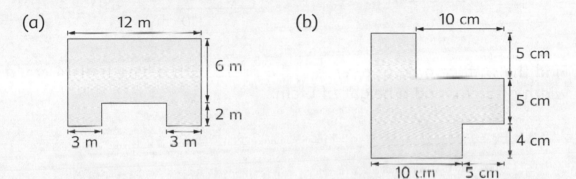

12 m

6 m

2 m

3 m   3 m

(b)

10 cm

5 cm

5 cm

4 cm

10 cm   5 cm

26. Find the area of each shaded triangle.

(a)

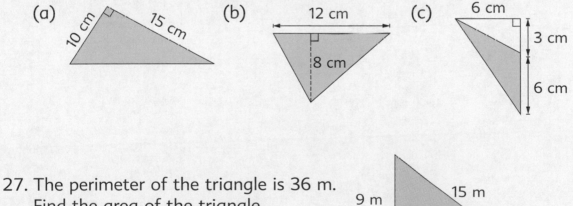

10 cm   15 cm

(b)

12 cm

8 cm

(c)

6 cm

3 cm

6 cm

27. The perimeter of the triangle is 36 m. Find the area of the triangle.

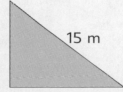

9 m   15 m

28. Find the shaded area of each rectangle.

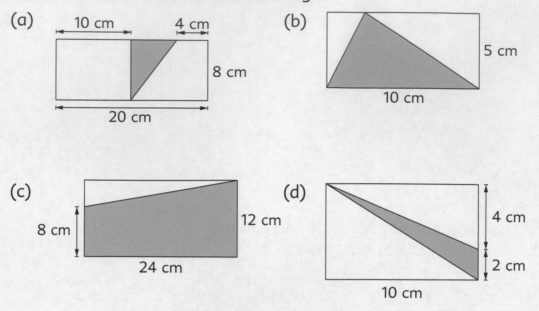

(a) 10 cm 4 cm 8 cm 20 cm

(b) 5 cm 10 cm

(c) 8 cm 24 cm 12 cm

(d) 4 cm 2 cm 10 cm

29. Find the surface area of a rectangular prism with a length of 14 cm, a width of 5 cm, and a height of 6 cm.

6 RATIO

1 Finding Ratio

David and John visited an art supply store. David bought 3 bottles of blue ink and 2 bottles of red ink.

The **ratio** of the number of bottles of blue ink to the number of bottles of red ink is 3 : 2.

We read the ratio 3 : 2 as **3 to 2**.

John bought 5 boxes of blue pens and 2 boxes of red pens.

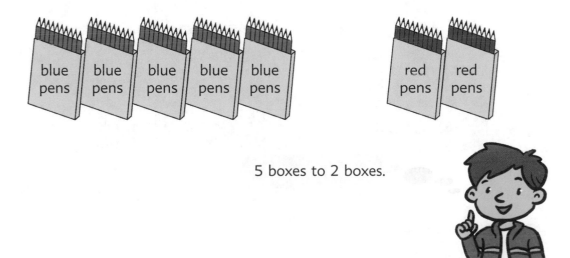

5 boxes to 2 boxes.

The **ratio** of the number of blue pens to the number of red pens is 5 : 2.

1. Ricardo mixed 3 cans of red paint with 1 can of white paint.

The ratio of the number of cans of red paint to the number of cans of white paint is 3 : 1.

The ratio of the number of cans of white paint to the number of cans of red paint is ☐ : ☐.

2.

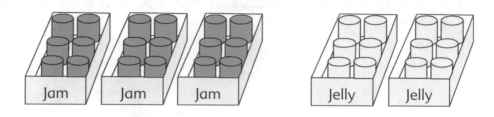

The ratio of the number of jars of jam to the number of jars of jelly is 3 : 2.

The ratio of the number of jars of jelly to the number of jars of jam is ☐ : ☐.

3.

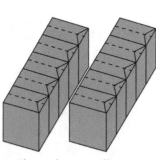

Chocolate milk   Strawberry milk

The ratio of the number of packets of chocolate milk to the number of packets of strawberry milk is ☐ : ☐.

The ratio of the number of packets of strawberry milk to the number of packets of chocolate milk is ☐ : ☐.

4.

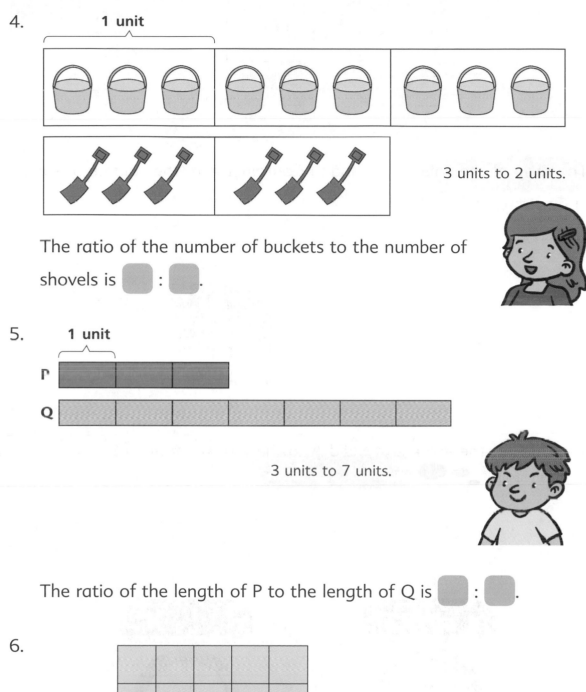

1 unit

3 units to 2 units.

The ratio of the number of buckets to the number of shovels is ☐ : ☐.

5.

1 unit

P

Q

3 units to 7 units.

The ratio of the length of P to the length of Q is ☐ : ☐.

6.

The ratio of the length of the rectangle to its width is ☐ : ☐.

7.

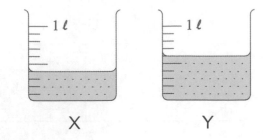

X   Y

The ratio of the volume of sand in Container X to the volume of sand in Container Y is ☐ : ☐.

8.

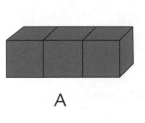
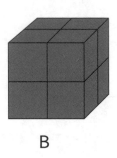

A   B

The ratio of the volume of Solid A to the volume of Solid B is ☐ : ☐.

9.

C   D

The ratio of the weight of Package C to the weight of Package D is ☐ : ☐.

  **Exercise 1, pages 129 - 130**

❷ Equivalent Ratios

John has 8 quarters and Peter has 12 quarters.

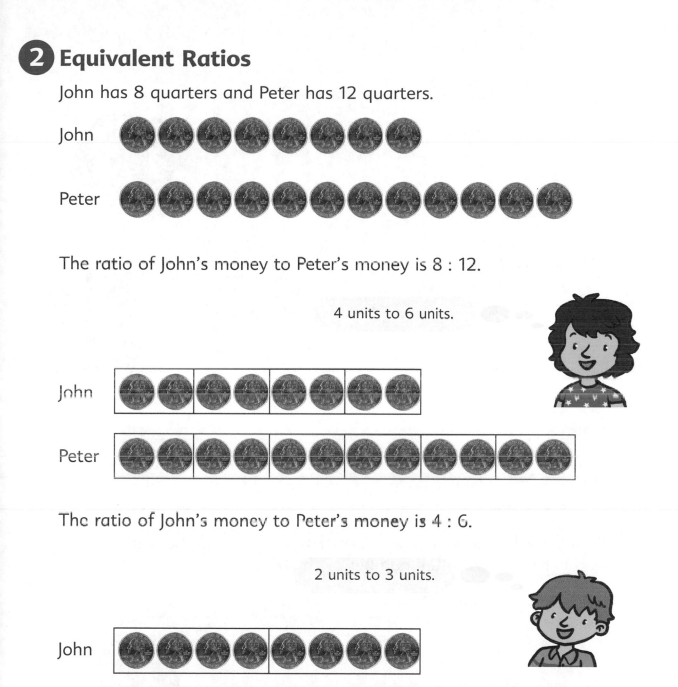

The ratio of John's money to Peter's money is 8 : 12.

4 units to 6 units.

The ratio of John's money to Peter's money is 4 : 6.

2 units to 3 units.

The ratio of John's money to Peter's money is 2 : 3.

8 : 12, 4 : 6 and 2 : 3 are **equivalent ratios**.

2 : 3 is a ratio in its simplest form.

1. Write each ratio in its simplest form.
   (a) 4 : 10

   4 : 10 = ☐ : ☐

   2 is a common factor
   of 4 and 10.
   Divide 4 and 10 by 2.

   ＡＴ : ＴＯ
   2   5

   (b) 12 : 18

   12 : 18 = ☐ : ☐

   6 is a common factor
   of 12 and 18.
   Divide 12 and 18 by 6.

   ＴＺ : ＴＢ
   2   3

2. Write each ratio in its simplest form.
   (a) 8 : 10   (b) 10 : 6
   (c) 6 : 24   (d) 21 : 14

3. There are 15 ducks and 12 chickens in a farm. Find the ratio of the
   number of ducks to the number of chickens.

   15 : 12 = ☐ : ☐

   Write the ratio 15 : 12
   in its simplest form.

   The ratio of the number of ducks to the number of chickens

   is ☐ : ☐.

Exercise 2, pages 131 - 132

4. There are 40 students in a class. 25 of them are boys. Find the ratio of the number of boys to the number of girls in the class.

Write the ratio 25 : 15 in its simplest form.

Number of girls = 40 − 25 = 15

Number of boys = 25

25 : 15 = ⬜ : ⬜

The ratio of the number of boys to the number of girls is ⬜ : ⬜.

5. The ratio of the length of Ribbon A to the length of Ribbon B is 7 : 4. If Ribbon A is 21 m long, find the length of Ribbon B.

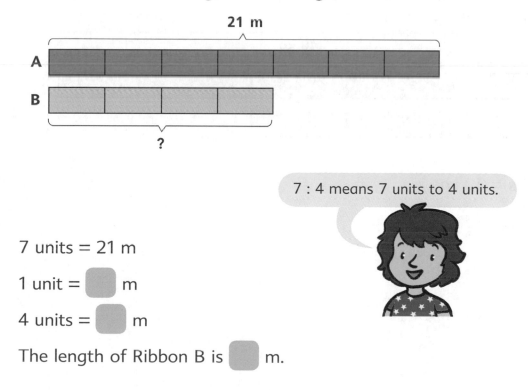

21 m

A

B

?

7 : 4 means 7 units to 4 units.

7 units = 21 m

1 unit = ⬜ m

4 units = ⬜ m

The length of Ribbon B is ⬜ m.

6. Siti and Mary shared $35 in the ratio 4 : 3. How much money did Siti receive?

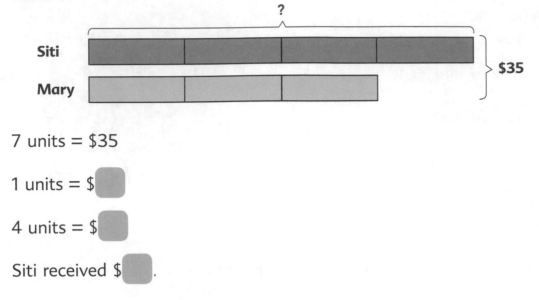

7 units = $35

1 units = $ ☐

4 units = $ ☐

Siti received $ ☐ .

7. The ratio of the weight of Package X to the weight of Package Y is 5 : 3. If the weight of Package X is 40 kg, find the total weight of the two packages.

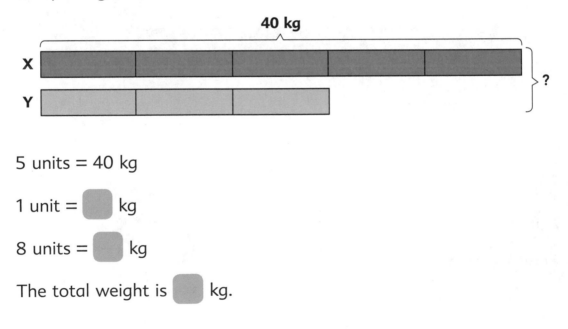

5 units = 40 kg

1 unit = ☐ kg

8 units = ☐ kg

The total weight is ☐ kg.

Exercise 3, pages 133 - 134

1.

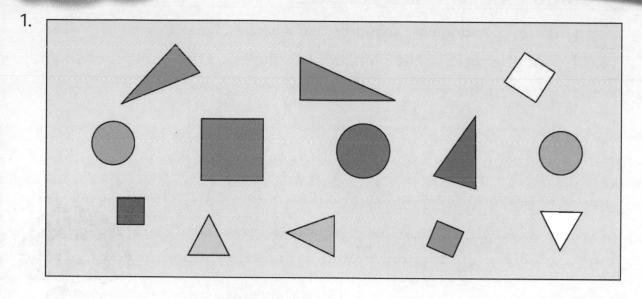

(a) Find the ratio of the number of circles to the number of triangles.
(b) Find the ratio of the number of triangles to the number of squares.

2. The length of a rectangle is 16 cm and its width is 12 cm. Find the ratio of the length of the rectangle to its width.

3. Ali won a cash prize of $50. He saved $35 and spent the rest. Find the ratio of the amount of money he saved to the amount of money he spent.

4. Brianne made pineapple drinks by mixing pineapple syrup and water in the ratio 2 : 7. If she used 4 liters of pineapple syrup, how much water did she use?

5. David cuts a rope 60 m long into two pieces in the ratio 2 : 3. What is the length of the shorter piece of rope?

6. The ratio of Adam's weight to John's weight is 6 : 5. If Adam weighs 48 kg, find John's weight.

7. The ratio of the number of boys to the number of girls is 2 : 5. If there are 100 boys, how many children are there altogether?

3 Combining Three Quantities

There are 12 triangles, 6 squares and 4 circles.

(a)   Find the ratio of the number of triangles to the number of squares.

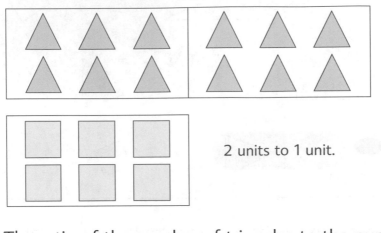

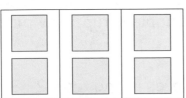

2 units to 1 unit.

The ratio of the number of triangles to the number

of squares is ⬜ : ⬜.

(b)   Find the ratio of the number of triangles to the number of squares to the number of circles.

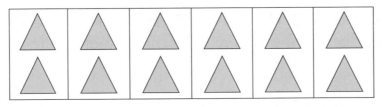

6 units to 3 units to 2 units.

The ratio of the number of triangles to the number of squares to

the number of circles is ⬜ : ⬜ : ⬜.

1. Write each ratio in its simplest form.

   (a) 12 : 6 : 4

   12 : 6 : 4 = ⬚ : ⬚ : ⬚

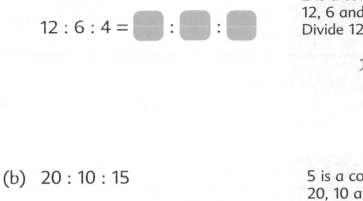

   2 is a common factor of 12, 6 and 4.
   Divide 12, 6 and 4 by 2.

   12 : 6 : 4
   6   3   2

   (b) 20 : 10 : 15

   20 : 10 : 15 = ⬚ : ⬚ : ⬚

   5 is a common factor of 20, 10 and 15.
   Divide 20, 10 and 15 by 5.

   20 : 10 : 15
   4   2   3

   Exercise 4, pages 135 - 136

2. 20 liters of water are poured into 3 buckets A, B and C in the ratio 2 . 3 . 5. Find the volume of water in Bucket C.

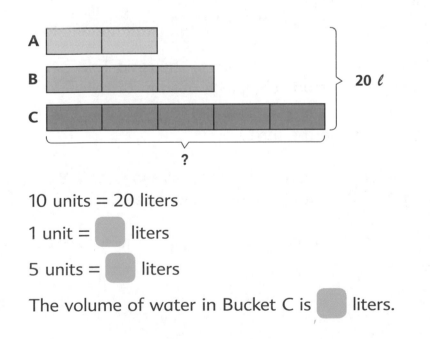

A

B   20 ℓ

C

?

10 units = 20 liters

1 unit = ⬚ liters

5 units = ⬚ liters

The volume of water in Bucket C is ⬚ liters.

Exercise 5, page 137

1. In a school, there are 24 female teachers and 10 male teachers. What is the ratio of the number of male teachers to the number of female teachers?

2. In a fruit orchard, there are 60 peach trees, 20 plum trees and 35 apricot trees. What is the ratio of the number of peach trees to the number of plum trees to the number of apricot trees?

3. Mrs. Bates cooked oatmeal by adding water to oatmeal in the ratio 3 : 1. If she used 12 cups of water, how many cups of oatmeal did she use?

4. In a swimming club, the ratio of the number of boys to the number of girls is 7 : 4. If there are 121 children in the swimming club, how many boys are there?

5. William has $120. Steve has $20 less than William. What is the ratio of Steve's money to William's money?

6. A pole, 90 cm long, is painted green, white and black in the ratio 3 : 4 : 2.
    (a) What length of the pole is painted green?
    (b) What length of the pole is painted black?

7. Cement, sand and stone chippings are mixed in the ratio 1 : 2 : 4. The total volume of sand and stone chippings used is 24 m³.
    (a) Find the volume of cement in the mixture.
    (b) Find the volume of sand in the mixture.

8. The ratio of David's weight to Ryan's weight to Ali's weight is 8 : 5 : 4. If Ryan weighs 30 kg, find the total weight of the 3 boys.

9. 3 boys share a sum of money in the ratio 5 : 3 : 2. If the smallest share is $30, find the biggest share.

REVIEW 6

1. What is the value of the digit 4 in each number?
   (a) 4650   (b) 16,409   (c) 427,055   (d) 4,256,000

2. The air distance between Singapore and London is 10,873 km. Round this distance to the nearest 100 km.

3. What is the missing number in each ▢ ?
   (a) $299 + \boxed{} = 605$ (b) $350 - \boxed{} = 186$
   (c) $8 \times \boxed{} = 736$ (d) $98 \div \boxed{} = 7$

4. Write the fractions represented by A, B and C in the simplest form.

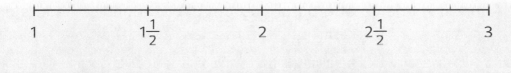

5. This figure is made up of congruent rectangles. What fraction of the figure is shaded?

6. (a) How many minutes is 6:25 p.m. before 7:00 p.m.?
   (b) How many hours and minutes are there between 10:45 a.m. and 2:10 p.m.?

7. Find the missing number.
   (a) $64 - (24 - 18) \times 10 = 64 - \boxed{}$
   (b) $3 \times 159 = (3 \times 160) - (3 \times \boxed{})$

8. Which expression will give the answer to the following problem?

   Sarah packed 128 cookies equally into 8 boxes. She gave 3 boxes away. How many cookies does she have left?

   $128 - 3 \times (128 \div 8)$ $5 \times (128 \div 8)$ $128 - 128 \div 8 \times 3$

9. Helen ate $\frac{1}{10}$ of a cake. She divided the remainder into 3 equal portions. What fraction of the cake was in each portion?

10. How many $\frac{1}{4}$'s are there in $\frac{3}{8}$?

11. How many $\frac{2}{5}$'s are there in $\frac{5}{8}$?

12. What is the area of each triangle?

(a)

(b)

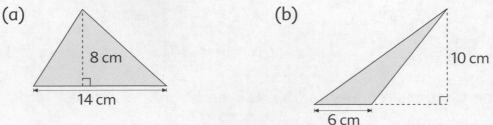

13. The figure is made up of a parallelogram and a triangle. Find its area.

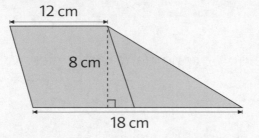

14. The figure is made up of a square and a triangle. If the area of the square is 64 cm², find the area of the triangle.

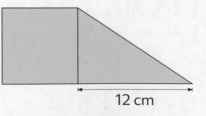

15. (a) What is the name of this solid?
    (b) How many faces does it have?

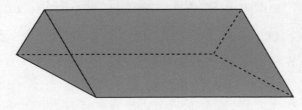

16. Find the surface area of the box.

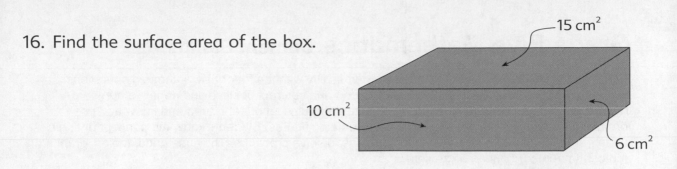

17. Find the perimeter and area of each figure.
    (All the lines meet at right angles.)
    (a)

    4 cm
    3 cm
    3 cm
    3 cm
    2 cm
    8 cm

    (b)
    8 cm   8 cm
         8 cm
    8 cm   12 cm
       8 cm

18. John and Peter share $180 in the ratio 3 : 2. How much more money does John receive than Peter?

19. The ratio of the length of a rectangular field to its width is 4 : 3. The length of the field is 20 m. Find its area and perimeter.

20. Sean, Ryan and John shared a sum of money in the ratio 3 : 4 : 5. If Sean received $30, what was the sum of money shared?

21. Michael bought a shirt with $\frac{2}{5}$ of his money. Then he bought a jacket which cost $5 more than the shirt. He spent $105 altogether. How much money did he have left?

22. Mrs. Wang spent $48 at the market. She spent $\frac{1}{6}$ of the money on vegetables and $\frac{1}{4}$ of the remainder on meat. The rest was spent on 2 kg of fish. Find the cost of 1 kg of fish.

23. A room is 6 m long and 5 m wide. $\frac{2}{3}$ of it is covered by a carpet.
    (a) Find the area of the carpet.
    (b) Find the cost of the carpet if 1 m² of it costs $80.

Review 6, pages 138 - 143

Grade Five Mathematics Content Standards

By the end of grade five, students increase their facility with the four basic arithmetic operations applied to fractions and decimals and learn to add and subtract positive and negative numbers. They know and use common measuring units to determine length and area and know and use formulas to determine the volume of simple geometric figures. Students know the concept of angle measurement and use a protractor and compass to solve problems. They use grids, tables, graphs, and charts to record and analyze data.

Number Sense

1.0 **Students compute with very large and very small numbers, positive integers, decimals, and fractions and understand the relationship between decimals, fractions, and percents. They understand the relative magnitudes of numbers:**

1.1 Estimate, round, and manipulate very large (e.g., millions) and very small (e.g., thousandths) numbers.

1.2 Interpret percents as a part of a hundred; find decimal and percent equivalents for common fractions and explain why they represent the same value; compute a given percent of a whole number.

1.3 Understand and compute positive integer powers of nonnegative integers; compute examples as repeated multiplication.

1.4 Determine the prime factors of all numbers through 50 and write the numbers as the product of their prime factors by using exponents to show multiples of a factor (e.g., $24 = 2 \times 2 \times 2 \times 3 = 2^3 \times 3$).

1.5 Identify and represent on a number line decimals, fractions, mixed numbers, and positive and negative integers.

2.0 **Students perform calculations and solve problems involving addition, subtraction, and simple multiplication and division of fractions and decimals:**

2.1 Add, subtract, multiply, and divide with decimals; add with negative integers; subtract positive integers from negative integers; and verify the reasonableness of the results.

2.2 Demonstrate proficiency with division, including division with positive decimals and long division with multi-digit divisors.

2.3 Solve simple problems, including ones arising in concrete situations, involving the addition and subtraction of fractions and mixed numbers (like and unlike denominators of 20 or less), and express answers in the simplest form.

2.4 Understand the concept of multiplication and division of fractions.

2.5 Compute and perform simple multiplication and division of fractions and apply these procedures to solving problems.

Algebra and Functions

1.0   Students use variables in simple expressions, compute the value of the expression for specific values of the variable, and plot and interpret the results:

1.1   Use information taken from a graph or equation to answer questions about a problem situation.

1.2   Use a letter to represent an unknown number; write and evaluate simple algebraic expressions in one variable by substitution.

1.3   Know and use the distributive property in equations and expressions with variables.

1.4   Identify and graph ordered pairs in the four quadrants of the coordinate plane.

1.5   Solve problems involving linear functions with integer values; write the equation; and graph the resulting ordered pairs of integers on a grid.

Measurement and Geometry

1.0   Students understand and compute the volumes and areas of simple objects:

1.1   Derive and use the formula for the area of a triangle and of a parallelogram by comparing each with the formula for the area of a rectangle (i.e., two of the same triangles make a parallelogram with twice the area; a parallelogram is compared with a rectangle of the same area by pasting and cutting a right triangle on the parallelogram).

1.2   Construct a cube and rectangular box from two-dimensional patterns and use these patterns to compute the surface area for these objects.

1.3   Understand the concept of volume and use the appropriate units in common measuring systems (i.e., cubic centimeter [cm^3], cubic meter [m^3], cubic inch [$in.^3$], cubic yard [$yd.^3$]) to compute the volume of rectangular solids.

1.4   Differentiate between, and use appropriate units of measures for, two- and three-dimensional objects (i.e., find the perimeter, area, volume).

2.0   Students identify, describe, and classify the properties of, and the relationships between, plane and solid geometric figures:

2.1   Measure, identify, and draw angles, perpendicular and parallel lines, rectangles, and triangles by using appropriate tools (e.g., straightedge, ruler, compass, protractor, drawing software).

2.2   Know that the sum of the angles of any triangle is 180° and the sum of the angles of any quadrilateral is 360° and use this information to solve problems.

2.3   Visualize and draw two-dimensional views of three-dimensional objects made from rectangular solids.

Statistics, Data Analysis, and Probability

1.0   Students display, analyze, compare, and interpret different data sets, including data sets of different sizes:

1.1   Know the concepts of mean, median, and mode; compute and compare simple examples to show that they may differ.

1.2   Organize and display single-variable data in appropriate graphs and representations (e.g., histogram, circle graphs) and explain which types of graphs are appropriate for various data sets.

1.3   Use fractions and percentages to compare data sets of different sizes.

1.4   Identify ordered pairs of data from a graph and interpret the meaning of the data in terms of the situation depicted by the graph.

1.5   Know how to write ordered pairs correctly; for example, (*x, y*).

Mathematical Reasoning

1.0   Students make decisions about how to approach problems:

1.1   Analyze problems by identifying relationships, distinguishing relevant from irrelevant information, sequencing and prioritizing information, and observing patterns.

1.2   Determine when and how to break a problem into simpler parts.

2.0   Students use strategies, skills, and concepts in finding solutions:

2.1   Use estimation to verify the reasonableness of calculated results.

2.2   Apply strategies and results from simpler problems to more complex problems.

2.3   Use a variety of methods, such as words, numbers, symbols, charts, graphs, tables, diagrams, and models, to explain mathematical reasoning.

2.4   Express the solution clearly and logically by using the appropriate mathematical notation and terms and clear language; support solutions with evidence in both verbal and symbolic work.

2.5   Indicate the relative advantages of exact and approximate solutions to problems and give answers to a specified degree of accuracy.

2.6   Make precise calculations and check the validity of the results from the context of the problem.

3.0   Students move beyond a particular problem by generalizing to other situations:

3.1   Evaluate the reasonableness of the solution in the context of the original situation.

3.2   Note the method of deriving the solution and demonstrate a conceptual understanding of the derivation by solving similar problems.

3.3   Develop generalizations of the results obtained and apply them in other circumstances.

GLOSSARY

Word	Meaning
approximation	The **approximation** of a number is the number obtained after we have rounded it to the nearest thousands, millions or billions. 2546 rounded to the nearest thousand is 3000. 2546 is **approximately** 3000.
billion	One **billion** is one thousand millions, or 1,000,000,000.
composite number	A **composite number** has factors other than 1 and itself. 6 is a composite number because its factors are 2 and 3 apart from 1 and itself.
equivalent ratios	**Equivalent ratios** are two or more ratios that have the same value. 1 : 2, 2 : 4 and 4 : 8 are **equivalent ratios**.
exponent	The **exponent** tells us how many times to multiply the base with itself. $$4^3 = 4 \times 4 \times 4$$ base **exponent**

Word	Meaning
factor	A **factor** is an exact divisor of a number. 4 is a **factor** of 16 since 16 is exactly divisible by 4.
greatest common factor	**Greatest common factor** is the common factor of two numbers that has the greatest value. Factors of 18: **1**, **2**, **3**, **6**, 9, 18 Factors of 24: **1**, **2**, **3**, 4, **6**, 8, 12, 24 1, 2, 3 and 6 are common factors of 18 and 24. 6 is the **greatest common factor** of 18 and 24.
improper fraction	An **improper fraction** has a value equal to, or greater than one. The numerator is equal to or greater than the denominator. $\frac{7}{4}$, $\frac{9}{7}$, $\frac{4}{3}$ are improper fractions.
like fractions	**Like fractions** are two or more fractions with common denominators. $\frac{4}{7}$ and $\frac{6}{7}$ are like fractions.

Word	Meaning
lowest common multiple	**Lowest common multiple** is the smallest number that is a common multiple of two numbers. Multiples of 2: 2, **4**, 6, **8**, 10, **12** ... Multiples of 4: **4**, **8**, **12** ... 4, 8, and 12 are common multiples of 2 and 4. 4 is the **lowest common multiple** of 2 and 4.
mixed number	A **mixed number** is made up of a whole number and a fraction. $1\frac{6}{7}$, $4\frac{8}{9}$, $3\frac{2}{5}$ are mixed numbers.
multiple	A **multiple** is the product of two factors of a number. 20 is a **multiple** of 2 since $2 \times 10 = 20$.
order of operations	The order in which we solve an expression containing two or more operation signs. Using the **order of operations**, multiplication and division is done first from left to right, followed by addition or subtraction from left to right.

Word	Meaning
period	Starting from the right, each group of 3 digits in a number forms a **period**. Each **period** is separated by a comma. In the number 7,465,243,082, '082' forms a **period**, '243' forms another **period** and so on.
prime factor	A **prime factor** is any factor of a number that is a prime number. The factors of 10 are 1, 2, 5 and 10. The **prime factors** of 10 are 2 and 5.
prime factorization	**Prime factorization** is the process of factoring a composite number into its prime factors.
prime number	A number is a prime number if: (a) it is greater than one, and (b) it has only and exactly two factors: 1 and itself. Example: 5 is a prime number because it is greater than 1, and its only two factors are 1 and 5 (itself).

Word	Meaning
ratio	**Ratio** is the comparison of two quantities expressed in the form x : y. Tom buys 5 pencils and 9 pens. The ratio of the number of pencils to the number of pens Tom buys is 5 : 9.

Index

Blank